BLINDSIDED

Parenting Through Emotional Crises, Developmental Challenges, and the Post-Pandemic Fallout

Jennifer Crossland, M.S., Ph.D.

Karen Mireau Books
Sonoma . California

ISBN: 978-1-968822-04-0

Cover Photos by Matt Crossland
Author Photos by Alicia Cervenka

Dedication

To my husband and best friend, Matt
who has always been my strongest support.
You have been my wonderful co-captain
as we have journeyed through life with our girls.

Contents

Preface

My name is Jennifer Crossland. I am the mother of three daughters, Caroline, age twenty-two, Julianne, age nineteen, and Abigail, age fourteen. I am also a clinical psychologist with thirty years of experience with children and teens who struggle with anxiety and depression, as well as individuals on the autism spectrum.

I am writing this book to offer you my personal story as a parent and my clinical experience as a psychologist. Each of my daughters has struggled in different ways where I have felt blindsided over the years. I hope to offer some ideas and guidance on how I weathered these storms as well as observations from my own private practice. There have been many parallels between my daughters' challenges, my training, and my clinical practice. My personal experience informs how I relate to parents, how I try to help parents cope through very difficult times, and how I help support parents in remaining hopeful.

My oldest daughter, Caroline, struggled with auditory processing issues at a very young age and went through multiple evaluations, Individualized Education Plan (IEP) meetings, and therapeutic support programs. My middle daughter, Jules, developed hearing loss after a routine ear surgery (myringotomy) and later developed celiac disease. My youngest daughter, Abby, struggled with social development during the pandemic and later some depression.

I have observed a palpable loss that my own daughters and so many children and teens experienced during and after the pandemic. I saw trauma and spiraling depression among teens I was working with. I saw parents feel helpless and hopeless as their child was losing ground in their academic goals and having significantly more dysregulated behavior without direct support in the online school modality. I saw how the pandemic has impacted our culture and communities and how the fallout continues now.

This is my story and I hope it will touch you or help you in some small way. My wish is that this book helps you feel empowered by offering strategies you can employ to support yourself and your children and hold on to hope no matter what challenges come your way.

—Jennifer Crossland
November, 2025

"Hope means finding light
in the darkness."

— *Desmond Tutu*

Chapter 1:

Advocating for Your Child

As I was sitting across the table at our public elementary school in Westchester County, New York, trying to take in all of the information, tears welled up in my eyes and I felt like I was getting flushed in the face. I heard the IEP (Individualized Education Plan) team[1] say that my daughter, Caroline, should leave the preschool that she loved and instead go to a different school, a special day program.

I had poured over all the testing results. This was the blessing and the curse of being both a psychologist and a parent when it came to my children. I had interpreted reports such as these many times. The data were inconsistent and therefore the findings were invalid. I knew the recommendations based on these findings did not fit for Caroline. I pushed my chair back from the table and could not speak. I looked around the room at the school team of providers who were recommending this placement, along with the special education director and the principal, and I realized that no one at the table making this recommendation about school placement had ever met, let alone evaluated, my daughter.

Our daughter's preschool teacher, special education itinerant teacher (SEIT)[2] and speech therapist were also at the table and made comments disagreeing with the recommendation. But, once they were pushed by the school

---

[1] Also known as the Student Services Team (SST) and Special Education Team. An Individualized Education Plan (IEP) includes a formal assessment by the public school with standardized testing, review of records and classroom observations. If the student qualifies with a disability, then a legally mandated plan is created for the student to receive individualized special education support services. This can be in the form of classroom support such as an aide to facilitate and support behavioral intervention as well as "pull out services" where the student has speech and language therapy, occupational therapy, social skills group and counseling.

[2] A SEIT, Special Education Itinerant Teacher, helps students in the classroom with skills like social communication, maintaining attention and other needs.

team, they fell silent. At one point, the special education coordinator left the room to call the special day school to see if they had a spot in their program. She returned saying that the school only had one spot left. Both my husband, Matt, and I felt incredible pressure to make a decision in the moment. We also knew the school they were recommending did not fit for our daughter and her needs.

Caroline was four years old. Matt very thoughtfully paused and pulled out a picture of our daughter from his wallet and placed it on the table. He said, "This is our daughter, Caroline. You don't know her but she is an amazing little girl. We are going to do everything we can to help her. This is who she is…"

Matt and I left the meeting that day feeling completely blindsided that the school had recommended pulling Caroline out of her current preschool program. We had been nothing but extremely vigilant in having her evaluated to receive early intervention services since the age of seventeen months old, starting with speech and occupational therapy (OT). In these very early years, my husband and I organized team meetings so that the speech therapist, OT, and preschool teacher could all talk together about goals, progress, etc. We understood that Caroline did not fit into a specific diagnosis which would justify a prototypical education plan.

As a psychologist, I had already attended many IEP meetings for clients and was very comfortable supporting and advocating for my clients and their parents to get appropriate school services. I was there to help advocate for the parents I worked with, to be a person who could push but still help the parents maintain a working relationship with the school. I could be another set of ears to hear the recommendations and support offered and also able to speak about the evaluation. I recognized how emotionally draining and difficult these meetings could be as I saw parents in tears or having to leave the room. Often these meetings would become adversarial or tense at best.

But now, I was sitting on the other side of the table as a very vulnerable mom. I knew how hard my husband and I had worked to support our daughter, collaborate with the team and organize play dates to practice her social skills. We observed all of her therapy services so we could replicate some of the support in our own home. It was exhausting. We were constantly worried. Now, as she was beginning her last year of preschool, the public school district was recommending a whole new level of support for her that we knew would drastically change her trajectory in life.

As I remember sitting with parents in IEP meetings for children I had evaluated or had met with for therapy, I can recall the tension in the room and parents' anxiety. The parents may feel that the IEP team doesn't truly understand who their child is because evaluations cannot completely capture the whole child. Parents feel vulnerable in these moments and very protective of their children. They want to advocate and get any services that may help their child. Oftentimes the school district wants to help and support but cannot provide certain services, and parents feel ill-equipped to navigate these waters, specifically knowing how to advocate for their child without burning a bridge. The education team often has a wealth of experience reading assessments and making recommendations for many children with different disabilities and challenges. However, the parents know their child in unique ways and need to bring that knowledge to the table to help individualize the plan based on their child's strengths and weaknesses.

One model that I have found helpful personally and clinically as I reflect back on my training is Dr. T. Berry Brazelton's Touchpoints and his Model of Development and Parent Assumptions (2003). I will weave in Brazelton's Touchpoints theory (1992), Guiding Principles and Parent Assumptions throughout this book.

Touchpoints Parent Assumptions

1. The parent is the expert on his/her child.

2. All parents have something critical to share at each developmental stage.

3. All parents have strengths.

4. All parents *want* to do well by their child.

5. All parents have ambivalent feelings.

6. Parenting is a process built on trial and error. (Brazelton & Sparrow, 2003)

For this chapter, I will focus on the first two points of Parent Assumptions. First, "The parent is the expert on his/her child." There is so much that parents bring to the table in their knowledge and understanding of their children. The education team can benefit tremendously from *partnering* with parents as a true "team" to present a more balanced and collaborative assessment.

Sometimes, however, parents can be left feeling like the audience or bystanders, not participating fully in the process and not being valued or heard. Even though I felt prepared for Caroline's meeting and understood the evaluation due to my clinical training and practice, I definitely felt like an outsider and not valued in my observations or input as a parent and "expert." To be able to contribute to these meetings, it is helpful to have specific observations ready to share (e.g., what your child is like on a playdate, with structure versus without structure, in certain settings like stores, birthday parties, etc.). The team is able to gather that information through history, but you as a parent have lived it and have important perspectives to share, and it is important that you speak up and contribute what you know.

The second Parent Assumption is that "All parents have something critical to share at each developmental stage" (Brazelton & Sparrow, 2003). Parents are in it! They see the ups and downs of their child in different contexts: on playdates, vacations, and birthday parties, and with family members and extended family members. Parents have a unique perspective and a lot to share at different Touchpoints in their child's life, as well as their own lives. There are critical stages not only for children but also for their parents. Vulnerable feelings come forward and parents can feel emotionally raw and overly protective of their children at these times.

I have observed that there are specific Touchpoints for parents of children with disabilities, such as holidays and birthdays, when they may be reflecting on gains and regressions with their child. Sometimes it is difficult for parents not to compare their child with disabilities to other neurotypical children at these milestones. It is helpful to anticipate these vulnerable times as a parent and try to engage in self-care, as well as ask for support from others. As a practitioner, being able to provide "preventive anticipatory guidance" (Brazelton & Sparrow), which is the core of Touchpoints, helps empower parents in being able to understand the potential emotional impact at these moments and how to create support around them.

For critical moments at education planning meetings, I always suggest that parents *bring someone* who can be an advocate and/or a listener to the IEP or 504[3] meeting whether it be a relative, wife, husband, partner or friend. I was deeply grateful that Matt was there at Caroline's IEP meeting to step back, try to re-center the meeting and regain control. If I had been there by myself, even with all of my experience and training, I would have likely shut down or become increasingly upset. This would not have been productive. The tone of the meeting ended up being centered around *caring* for our daughter and helping her be successful in a school environment, instead of only looking at numbers and statistics and being prescriptive in recommendations. It was important for our IEP team to think outside the box for our daughter. Unfortunately, most parents do not feel this sense of empowerment at the meeting or throughout the process.

In my work with families who have had a child with a diagnosis of autism, I often try to help both parents process the diagnosis, what it means, and to help them understand that there is a

---

[3] A 504 evaluation and plan is for students who do not qualify for special education services. The process is less formal and involved than an IEP. Often teachers complete questionnaires, observations, and the team reviews other records. The accommodations are generally focused on the classroom setting, such as providing a multimodal curriculum to the student, preferential seating, and extra time on tests and projects.

grief process and readjustment process. Some studies have shown that parents of children with disabilities, including those with autism or ADHD (Attention Deficit Hyperactivity Disorder), have as much as a 75 percent higher relative risk of divorce compared to parents of children without disabilities (Kvist et al., 2013). Each partner may have a different view and find themself in a different place with processing the diagnosis and their life ahead. Couples may feel completely exhausted and overwhelmed and not able to lean on each other. I always try to turn these couples toward family and friends who want to help and give them respite. At my local church, we offered respite nights for parents who needed a night out and a break from all of the stress of caring for their child. As a community, we need to be there for each other and help alleviate some of the burden on these families.

Since there is so much information being presented (test results, observations, recommendations, etc.), it can also be extremely helpful to have an expert advocate sitting with you. Parents can invite an outside counselor or therapist to attend their child's IEP meetings. It is helpful to get another person's professional perspective because they can track different pieces that the parents may have missed or could not fully process. It can also be wonderful to see the face of a support person like a therapist at the table because it can help decrease stress. Often I have had parents compare the meeting to a marathon where they feel completely exhausted and drained afterward. Different providers speak about their observations and their specific evaluations, taking turns going around the table presenting information. Sometimes the report can be over ten pages long! Parents are supposed to receive the comprehensive report ahead of time to review, but it is very difficult to digest everything, process emotionally, and then advocate for your child in the context of the meeting. [4]

---

[4] Over the past twenty-one years in private practice, I have noticed a shift in tone in IEP meetings with school teams partnering more with parents, soliciting their observations of their child and checking in with them to see if the evaluation results

It is really important that parents know they have resources. You can get guidance and understanding of your rights under I.D.E.A. (Individual with Disabilities Act) through Parent Center Hub (www.parentcenterhub.org/iep). There are chapters all over the United States that have experts on staff to talk through your rights regarding educating children who have disabilities. Unfortunately, I was unaware of this resource when I was going through the process for my daughter.

It is important to note that the initial IEP meeting is often the most overwhelming with all the test results and various providers presenting their findings and making recommendations. It is good to know that usually you do not need to make a decision about the education plan on the spot because parents sometimes feel pressure to agree to make decisions in the moment. As a parent, *you can take time* after the meeting to digest the information, get perspective or consultation, and then move forward with the recommendations or advocate for additional or modified services. In addition, if you feel a sense of urgency to get support going for your child, particularly if they have a very significant need, it is important *to stay proactive with the team* in following up on implementation of services after the meeting.

As you move through the IEP meetings and follow-up dialogue, the process will come to feel much less emotional and intense. It is important to understand that there will be ups and downs, times when you will feel overwhelmed and raw, and times when you will feel more momentum, and more empowerment. This is not a smooth, linear process. I found that my husband and I often

---

and observations "fit" for the parent. Despite the best intentions, however, it is difficult to have an open-ended, interactive discussion between school staff and parents at the meeting due to time constraints. All the providers at the table have to efficiently present observations, test results and recommendations, and often the principal of the school is the facilitator who keeps the meeting moving along. I have noticed with Zoom IEP meetings (since the pandemic), there seems to be more sharing of information and less overwhelm for parents versus sitting at a table with the entire school team. Perhaps this feels a little less intimidating for parents and there is more openness in this modality.

"see-sawed" emotionally: when one of us felt more energized and encouraged, the other felt more discouraged. We realized that it is critically important to take turns carrying the burden for each other. Also, you are in a long-term relationship with the school. So it is important to build bridges with the team while also advocating and caring for your child.

After Caroline's IEP meeting that day and a lot of thought and research, Matt and I ultimately rejected the special day program recommendation. While a program like this is very helpful to many children and families, it was not the right fit for Caroline given her strengths and weaknesses. Instead, Matt and I pushed to increase services at her current preschool program. We had her SEIT come into the classroom additional days each week to help facilitate social communication for Caroline. We also increased her speech and language services. I organized more playdates and social activities for Caroline in order for her to "practice" what she was learning in her social communication.

Caroline continued to work so hard with all of these providers and Matt and I continued to help her generalize these skills to the home environment. All of this led to Caroline starting kindergarten at our public elementary school in a collaborative classroom program where there was a general education teacher, special education teacher and the students were grouped in pods based on their needs and for individualized attention. This was a revolutionary program that helped Caroline in so many ways and helped prepare her to join a general education class with pull out services[5] the following year.

In summary, advocating for your child is a process. It is a process of adjusting to new information about your child, learning of a potential DSM-V (Diagnostic and Statistical Manual-5th edition) diagnosis, and possibly hearing that he or she is now classified by the

---

[5] Pull out services are support services in the IEP where students are pulled out of the classroom for one on one or group work in areas such as speech and language therapy, social pragmatics, occupational therapy, social skills group and counseling.

school as needing special education. Often this in and of itself can be very difficult to accept for parents, even if those delivering the news are experts and supportive. It is another process to go forward and try to assimilate the new information about your child. They are still the child you know and love. They have not changed, but there can be fear, anger, and sadness as you try to incorporate everything into your daily life. We will explore this further in the next chapter along with psychological adjustment to disability. Here are some important tips to take away as you embark on the process of working with the school during the IEP or 504 process:

1. Do not have unrealistic expectations of yourself and what you can process during the initial IEP meeting.

2. Bring an advocate to the meeting to help support and process information for you.

3. Try to bring in observations of your child in settings other than school (e.g., at home, playdates, vacations, birthday parties, etc.). You see your child in many different contexts and are the expert on your child!

4. Give yourself time to digest the information after the meeting.

5. Remember that you do not need to make a decision in the meeting and it may be too overwhelming to process everything. Even as an experienced psychologist who does psychoeducational assessments and reviewed Caroline's assessment to prepare prior to the meeting, I was completely overwhelmed.

6. Consult your local Parent Center Hub for more information on your legal rights and get information and support if needed: www.parentcenterhub.org/iep

7. Be proactive in following up with the education team. Understand the timeline to sign paperwork and check back in to see when services will begin. This is very important! Also it is critical to find out how frequently you will receive progress reports, reviews, or updates and what the mode of communication will be with teachers and providers.

8. Enlist support from your spouse or partner, family, friends, therapist, psychologists, even clergy to share the burden of the process and to allow for another's perspective.

9. Breathe and be kind to and patient with yourself!

Chapter 2:

❧

Dealing with Doubt, Blame, Guilt and Anger

During our diagnostic journey and school planning with Caroline, our middle daughter, Julianne (Jules), had to have two bilateral myringotomies (surgical ear tube installations) to address continuous ear infections and residual fluid in her ears. Caroline previously had the same surgeries on her eardrums due to the same medical concerns, so this was not new territory for us. Since my husband and I wanted to be vigilant with Jules and not have her experience any issues around sensory processing, speech or otherwise, we moved quickly on the surgery. Jules' first surgery was just under one year of age and seemed to be successful. After the second surgery at around two, however, the perforations in her eardrums stayed open and did not heal. We were completely blindsided and felt very concerned.

When Jules' otolaryngologist (ENT) explained to me that her eardrums still had perforations, he also explained that a tiny hole in her left eardrum that was present at the second surgery combined with the hole where the tube was placed. This caused a bigger perforation that was much more concerning. I was incredibly worried. He then explained that this could cause hearing loss since the eardrum needed to be intact and vibrate to hear different sounds and frequencies. Immediately, the doctor instructed me to take Jules into a sound booth in their office for an audiological evaluation. I could feel my heart racing and had a terrible feeling in the pit of my stomach. Everything seemed to be happening so fast.

I sat in the sound booth with Julianne sitting on my lap. She had to face away from me so that I could not cue her when certain sounds were presented. I quickly realized that she was not responding to the audiologist, who was projecting different sounds into the booth for her to respond to. There were toys and other objects for her to point to as the audiologist instructed her at different volumes. She was also instructed to raise her hand when she could hear different sounds. I could easily hear the sounds that were being projected into the booth. My heart sank as they tried multiple sounds at different frequencies with no response. I was heartbroken. She was only three. I was tearing up and did not know what to do next. I tried to ask questions but I knew I was about to break down crying. I thought to myself, "Does that mean she has permanent hearing loss? How could this have happened?"

The audiologist recommended that we schedule a full audiological evaluation to determine the severity of Jules' hearing loss, receptive and expressive language functioning and general speech. This appointment would last several hours. We quickly scheduled this evaluation and felt like our whole world was being turned upside down.

Later, as we were driving into New York city for this evaluation, we knew that the results could change Jules' life and ours in a traumatic way. Matt and I walked into the waiting room, where several other parents who had children with hearing loss and hearing aids also waited. It was difficult to cover up our anxiety in front of Jules and hold back the tears. I kept asking myself, "How did we get here?" Jules did not have any kind of disability before her surgery, and now it looked like she did.

Matt and I spent several hours in interviews and the evaluation. The audiologist involved us in playing with Jules as she watched behind a one-way mirror. She gave us commands in what to say to her to cue certain responses. Then the audiologist took a turn to evaluate her auditory comprehension and expression in a more structured way. She conducted this part of the evaluation in both a direct, face-to-face modality and also from behind, where Jules could not see her to be cued or read her lips.

This part was the most devastating. Matt and I stood behind the one-way mirror and our hearts sank. We could see that she was not responding. We felt so helpless and knew what this meant. She had significant conductive hearing loss. which can be caused when trauma or an accident results in sound waves being unable to reach the inner ear.

This is in contrast to sensorineural hearing loss, which can be present at birth or at a very young age due to illness, drug toxicity, genetics and other causes (Tanna et al., 2023). In Jules' case, there was no damage to the hair cells within the inner ear, the vestibulocochlear nerve, or the brain's central processing centers

(Yoho et al., 2023). Jules had moderate conductive hearing loss in her right ear and severe conductive hearing loss in her left ear (due to the two holes combining). We felt hopeless and helpless.

We felt like our car ride back to our home in Westchester took forever, but we knew the road ahead of us with Jules would be much longer. This was unchartered territory for us as we had not had a child with a physical disability. We felt confused and did not know where to begin. I knew that she would need an IEP evaluation, speech and language therapy and hearing aids, but I was stuck emotionally and felt paralyzed by the news. Even though we had gone through the process of seeing the ENT a number of times and had repeated audiological evaluations, including the comprehensive evaluation, I felt like I was in shock. I think I still hoped for the ears to heal on their own or for Jules to magically, somehow, suddenly not have any hearing loss.

When individuals try to adjust to medical illness or disability, they experience different phases and a range of emotional responses. Oftentimes, this process is equated to the Grief Process that Elizabeth Kubler-Ross so famously brought to the public in 1969 in her seminal book, On Death and Dying. Livneh and Antonak (2018) propose another model that discusses different triggered responses as people adjust to chronic illness and disability (CID). These phases are not necessarily linear and sequential and people move back and forth through them depending on different events, such as additional evaluations, surgeries, new treatments, therapy, medication, etc.

In this chapter, we will discuss Livneh and Antonak's model, which is based on how an *individual with an illness or disability* is coping through the phases. In our situation with Jules having a sudden, unexpected disability at a very young age, my husband and I were the ones going through these phases instead of her. It turns out that parents of young children with disabilities move through these phases in place of their children, who likely may not be able to process all that is happening to them.

Livneh and Antonak's phases of coping with CID are as follows:

1. Shock - Short-lived reaction that marks the initial experience following the onset of a traumatic injury, diagnosis or chronic disability or disease. It is characterized by psychic numbness, cognitive disorganization, and dramatically decreased mobility or disrupted mobility and speech.

2. Anxiety - Characterized by a panic-like response to initial sensing of the nature and magnitude of the event. It can be accompanied by confused thinking, cognitive flooding, and a multitude of physiological symptoms.

3. Denial - Regarded as a defense mechanism mobilized to ward off anxiety and other threatening emotions. It can include wishful thinking and unrealistic expectations.

4. Depression - Reflects the realization of the permanency, magnitude and future implications associated with the loss and chronicity of the illness or disability. It can also be associated with despair, hopelessness, helplessness, isolation and stress.

5. Anger/Hostility - This can be internalized (self-directed feelings and behaviors of resentment, bitterness, guilt and self-blame) or it can be externalized (environment-directed retaliatory feelings and behavior).

6. Adjustment - Reorganization, reintegration or reorientation. This includes reconciliation of the condition's impact and chronic or permanent nature, affective acceptance or internalization of oneself as a person with CID (including a new self-concept), renewed life

values and search for new meanings, and active pursuit of personal and social goals, with negotiation of obstacles in pursuit of these goals (pp. 80-81).

In our situation, Jules was only three years old and never seemed to be in shock, denial, depression, or anger. This was merely a small obstacle where she had to go to audiological evaluations and speech and language therapy and wear hearing aids. But for us as parents, it was incredibly raw and devastating. I was grateful that she could not fully comprehend what this disability might mean for her long-term. At Julianne's developmental stage, she was not able to employ future-oriented thinking, and this was a blessing. Jules remained very positive and resilient throughout this time. In contrast, Matt and I viscerally experienced all of these phases very painfully and deeply.

Throughout the evaluations, trying to process and assimilate new information, I felt very overwhelmed and just tried to get through the process. I was not yet able to reflect on the big picture, what was truly happening, and my overwhelming anxiety and sadness. I definitely experienced "shock" and my own paralysis after that final audiological evaluation. I had the information about her hearing deficits and need for hearing aids but I had tremendous difficulty processing any of it. All I knew was that I was supposed to move forward to schedule a hearing aid fitting and a new audiological evaluation with her ongoing therapist, who would be working with her and her school for accommodations.

As I struggled to do this, I remember feeling the "anxiety" and extreme overwhelm. It was difficult to take in what I needed to do with her hearing aids: how to test them on a daily basis, when to have her wear them and take a break, how to continue to protect her open ear drums with plugs during bathing and swimming, how to proceed with helping her at home with speech and cues, and how to strengthen her understanding with hearing loss. I definitely felt flooded with all this new information and was not sure how to juggle everything. At the same time, I had to stay vigilant and involved in

Caroline's school support services and outside support services (speech and language therapy and occupational therapy) every day.

I remember waking up many nights feeling panicked and hoping it was all a nightmare. I also tried to recount everything that happened and how it happened, step-by-step. I kept trying to dig down and see how we could have avoided damaging her ears and what I could have done differently. I sought out support from a psychotherapist. I could not shake the feeling that we had caused this disability with the decision to have Jules go through the second surgery. At the time, we had known that for Caroline, constant fluid in her ears negatively impacted her visual-spatial skills and auditory processing, and surgery was helpful. But for Jules, we knew now that complications from the surgery may have caused conductive hearing loss and a permanent disability. I tried to remind myself that we could not have known that her ears would not heal. This was extremely rare, and her ENT had never seen both eardrums fail to heal in his medical experience over many years. But I kept feeling I should have known this would happen and I felt completely responsible, a sense that created constant anxiety.

I also experienced the following phase, "denial," but more in the form of wishful thinking. I kept hoping and praying that Jules' ears would spontaneously close. I researched different foods that had healing power (with vitamin K) and wondered about holistic approaches to help her heal. I continued to hear that the only way to fix her eardrums was through a risky surgery called a tympanoplasty that takes skin from behind the ear externally and patches the eardrum. But there was no guarantee that this surgery would work and the skin would patch successfully onto the drum. Sometimes there is scar tissue, which can make things worse. In addition, the way that a doctor has to remove the skin from behind the ear involves taking the ear partially off and reattaching it. This can result in the ears not looking symmetrical anymore. I knew for a girl who would be very self-conscious of her looks one day, this could be very impactful. Most importantly, there was no certainty that Jules's

16

hearing would improve. This was the thought that kept me up at night, my heart racing, and feeling panicked all the time.

I definitely experienced "depression" in this next phase. I found myself trying to explain to friends and family how this all happened. Every time I talked about it, I felt that I was reliving the experience, especially the helplessness. I moved in and out of feeling isolated even though I had friends and family, particularly my husband, who supported me and our journey through this. I did not feel like I could really identify with the hearing-impaired community since this occurred through a physical procedure, the surgery. I resisted getting connected with any support groups or reaching out to other parents of children who were hearing impaired. Ironically, Caroline's speech and language therapist had twin sons who were deaf with sensorineural hearing loss and I would listen to her story. Yet I resisted becoming emotionally connected to her experience.

In the midst of all of this, we decided to move from New York to California. We felt that Caroline, in particular, would really benefit from a "reset" with a more inclusive culture for children with special needs. In addition, the weather seemed to negatively impact Caroline during the harsh New York winters. We observed significant regression in her development during the winter months when she could not go outside to run around, play and get sunshine. My husband and I also wondered how the move would impact Jules. We knew she would get good medical care and were looking at school districts that were "Centers of Excellence" for children with special needs.

I knew we had to have an IEP evaluation for her hearing loss to get accommodations in the classroom, but I felt like I had no patience for this. We had been through this before for Caroline, and now we had to do this again for Jules for a disability that may have been preventable. During this next phase of "anger/hostility," I experienced very intense emotions of self-directed blame, guilt, bitterness and resentment. I kept asking "why?" and "how?" At the end of the day, I felt I should have known and could have prevented this disability. Why did we move so fast on these surgeries? We could have taken the "wait and see" approach. We were also learning that the tympanoplasty could not be done until Jules was at least nine or ten years old, so she would have hearing aids and open eardrums for the next six or seven years at least.

In the meantime, there was constant worry about her getting water inside her eardrums. We had to continue to use ear plugs in the bath, shower and pools, and we had to be hypervigilant about making sure she did not get any debris in her ears. One time, we were at the beach and she was knocked over by a wave before we put her ear plugs in and a cap on her head. Jules ended up getting sand inside her ear, which caused an ear infection and a trip to urgent care during our vacation. We had to postpone our flight until we knew she was safe to fly. When people would ask me about her hearing issues, sometimes acquaintances or people I did not know well, I found myself getting defensive. I was projecting my sense of anger at myself onto them. I also found myself getting resentful of seeing children who had no apparent disabilities, those without hearing aids, with no IEPs. I felt they had no clue how fortunate they were.

This phase of anger carried over into the school environment as well. Jules not only had to wear hearing aids, she also had to be connected to a microphone that the teacher wore during class. The teacher had to be vigilant about wearing it so Jules could clearly hear her speaking to her and to the class. Otherwise, all the other sound was amplified in the class, such as chairs moving, other students talking, and ambient sounds, if she only had her hearing aids on. This would supposedly help her not get distracted by all the other sounds and focus on classroom instruction from the teacher, the most important sound she should hear. Of course, this was not perfect. The teacher had to remember to turn on her microphone while managing all of the other students. This is not an easy task in a preschool or kindergarten class. The teacher also had to remember to turn off her microphone when not instructing. All the while, Jules always seemed to be smiling and humming (we think this helped her

18

maintain her attention in class) and willing to adapt to whatever came her way. While she seemed happy, I struggled with the reality that I may have a daughter who would never hear again without a risky surgery to repair the eardrums.

When we moved to California (the San Francisco Bay Area), the school district had to implement Jules' IEP just as they did with Caroline, however, Jules was still in her last year of preschool at a church so she was not in a public school. We had to trust that the teacher would use the microphone appropriately. Jules had speech and language therapy as part of her IEP, which felt pointless as she had completely normal articulation and comprehension as long as she was wearing her hearing aids.

Often when people experience transitions and milestones (e.g., moving, birthdays), it can unearth difficult feelings of grief again, which I definitely felt. I also found myself reliving the "why", which was always accompanied by anger. I blamed myself. I blamed the doctor who did the surgery. I even scheduled a very difficult phone call with him pointedly asking how this could have happened. Since he saw another small hole in the left ear drum, why did he place another tube? He had explained several times that he inserted another tube in a different location away from the very small hole that he saw in Julianne's eardrum during the surgery. She was already under anesthesia and he used his best medical judgment. The reality was that the small hole in her left ear drum would have likely gotten bigger over time anyway.

I knew that reliving all of this was not helpful, but it was incredibly difficult for me to let go of the anger, blame and guilt. At the end of the day, I was her mother, and Matt and I jointly decided to have the second surgery. Of course, I did *not* ask myself more compassionate, realistic questions like: "How could I have known? How could this possibly be my fault? How could I personally have caused this to happen?" Those were all questions my psychotherapist would challenge me on. It was really hard, though, for me to reflect on the trauma this way. Having a therapist to support me and my

19

internal struggles with guilt, resentment and feeling out of control as a parent was undeniably critical for my adjustment throughout all these phases, particularly in dealing with my anger. I had to let go of my magical thinking that I had some level of control in all of this. I also leaned on my friends, family, faith and prayer.

The last phase of "reorganization, reintegration or reorientation" was ongoing and continues even now at different phases of my daughters' lives. I knew that I had to "reconcile" myself with the hearing loss and possibly permanent disability. That acknowledgement brought up so much sadness in me, but we continued on with our move across the country. Somehow I felt that reorganizing our family in a new setting, a new state and new culture with new medical care and providers, might make a difference. I was very hopeful that this indeed would be the case for Caroline. With Jules and her hearing loss and new IEP, I could not be certain. Jules' ENT in New York referred us to see a world-renowned ENT at Stanford, who was very skilled in tympanoplasty and other surgical procedures and treatments with the ear. I still did not embrace social support groups for parents of hearing-impaired children, however I felt like I had to maintain hope that the surgery one day (possibly six years from now) would restore Jules' hearing.

The idea of "reorientation" resonates since as a family, we were moving into a new community to forge a new identity (in a way) and a new start. Prior to moving and settling on the community, I did a lot of research on school districts. I knew we had to feel confident that the school district had the right mindset for our girls, who both came into the district with IEPs. We had to feel assured that the school would replicate and carry out their IEPs, provide accommodations and be inclusive and supportive. I met with principals and directors of special education. It took only a few minutes of speaking with them to know if the school district would provide this inclusive culture and prioritized supporting students with special needs, and the school system we finally chose had everything we were looking for.

When we moved, we did not know anyone except for a few of Matt's work colleagues, but his brother and sister-in-law lived about an hour away in the Bay Area, and I felt at peace with our decision to move and embrace the new community around us. We felt welcomed right away, and I started to meet friends who would be critical in this new part of our family journey.

Even with that sense of optimism, however, we also had a difficult time finding all new providers and doctors to work with Jules and our family. I felt I was back to reliving the trauma again because I had to tell all the doctors what happened to Jules and her ears and her medical history. Since I was meeting new friends, they also had questions and recommendations of who to see and who not to see for ENTs. In addition, I had to stay proactive about Jules' and Caroline's IEPs to ensure they were continuing to receive the services they needed. I also had to resist getting back in the cycle of blame and anger again.

As I moved through these phases, in a non-linear way and sometimes reverting back to old phases I thought I had resolved, I had to learn to be patient with myself. The Touchpoints Framework incorporates the ideas that development is not linear and there are both disruptions and gains in development (Brazelton & Sparrow, 2003). I would argue that this concept mirrors a parent's adjustment to their child's disability as they experience disruptions, periods of disorganization, and setbacks. These times are woven into gains and successes in a child's development, as well as parents' occasional celebrations and taking deep breaths of respite when things appear to be going well. The process is multidimensional and needs to be viewed in the larger realm of family networks and other external systems, such as school, medical team, and community support, including faith entities, friends and family.

In our family's situation, we had just moved from across the country. We were starting over and I needed to be very present for all my family members as we made this transition. We enjoyed meeting new friends, the California culture of spending so much time outside, and warm September and October evenings with new friends and family visiting. Everyone seemed very supportive. We chose the Bay Area in large part due to the weather because we knew that our girls would be at their best in a warm, sunny climate, and not sick and indoors as much in the winter months. In fact, we ruled out other climates because we could see this impact on our girls in New York.

In our new setting, I felt like I could breathe and let go of some of the anger and self-blame. I thought that maybe after all the trauma we felt blindsided by back in New York, (Caroline's evaluations, IEP, school struggle with finding the right kind of integrated classroom and Jules' hearing loss and new IEP), this new start would diminish some of my sadness. The place was unfamiliar and did not carry those memories along with it. Could we start over? It was a new era, and I was trying to be hopeful.

In summary, based on my personal and clinical experience, I believe that the process of coping with a disability can be interwoven with Touchpoints theory to illuminate not only how children develop, but also how parents adjust to disability in their child. I will unpack the Touchpoints theory and Guiding Principles in the next chapter. These principles are helpful to not only practitioners, but also to families who may want to make sure this perspective is included in their support team's way of working. As we talked about in this chapter, dealing with doubt, blame, guilt and anger around a child's disability can be overwhelming and life changing for parents. Here are some helpful points to remember during the coping process:

1. Adjustment to a disability is a complex, non-linear process. This is the case for parents as well as children, depending on the child's age.

2. Livneh and Atonak's model calls these phases of coping with a disability: Shock, Anxiety, Denial, Depression, Anger and Adjustment.

3. It is important to give yourself permission to go in and out of these phases and remember that some phases will come back and emotions will resurface and feel raw at times.

Chapter 3:

⤜

Developing Coping Skills for Fight or Flight:
Being the Calm in the Eye of the Storm

During the process of evaluating the extent of hearing loss for Julianne, I had many moments of "fight or flight." We had moved to California and were trying to adapt to a new life in many ways, however, that panicky feeling still accompanied the persistent, nagging question of "why" and "how could I have helped prevent this?" I found myself waking up in the middle of the night in a cold sweat with my heart racing. I frantically scoured medical journals to see if there was anything I could do, any stone left unturned, to increase the probability of her ears healing. I felt like I had to spend time online as much as possible, looking for any other solutions, homeopathic treatments, anything. I wanted the nightmare to be over and still felt frantic and heartbroken. I remember even going to exercise at the gym and crying while I was on the bike. I would try to avoid eye contact with people so they would not see my sadness or stress. I felt like I was going through some level of post-traumatic stress disorder (PTSD). Even though so many of the reminders of the challenge we had been through in New York were no longer present, the pain and anxiety continued.

⤜

During this time of settling into our new lives in California and trying to establish a new normal, I leaned on the Touchpoints Guiding Principles. These principles are primarily intended to guide practitioners who are working with families through their children's healthy, neurotypical development. Now, as a parent having experienced my own trauma, I found that Touchpoints helped me cope and adjust to my daughter's disability.

In this chapter, I will discuss the Touchpoints Guiding Principles, which are addressing the psychologist aiding the family. I will also go a step further to explain how I believe that this perspective can be adapted to parents going through their journey with their child's diagnosis and adjustment to disability:

Touchpoints Guiding Principles

1. Value and understand the relationship between you and the parent.

2. Use the behavior of the child as your language.

3. Recognize what you bring to the interaction.

4. Be willing to discuss matters that go beyond your traditional role.

5. Value passion wherever you find it.

6. Focus on the parent-child relationship.

7. Look for opportunities to support mastery.

8. Value disorganization and vulnerability as an opportunity.

The premise of Touchpoints represents a significant paradigm shift from psychology's traditional focus on weaknesses or deficits to a positive or growth model (Brazelton & Sparrow, 2003). Following the first Principle, "value and understand the relationship between you and the parent," instead of being prescriptive, the practitioner is collaborative and empathic, going beyond his/her role rather than having only objective involvement with strict boundaries. As a mother going through an adjustment process with both Caroline and Jules, I definitely responded better when the professionals used the positive approach. I did not want either of my daughters to be defined by a disability or to lose hope as a parent and ultimately feel powerless. Similarly, as a practicing psychologist, I tried to value and understand the relationship between the parents and me because I knew that a positive dynamic could truly empower them. It was not my job to be prescriptive and tell them what they *should* do, which only makes them feel more dependent on professionals for the right answer. I knew the feeling of waiting on medical professionals for answers on what our next step would be, and it left me with an unconstructive feeling of helplessness.

The second Touchpoints Principle, "use the behavior of the child as your language," is important in establishing trust and rapport with parents. It also shows that you are observing how the child is communicating with and relating to the parent. I recognized when other practitioners were talking about either Caroline or Jules in this behavior-focused way, and it made me feel comfortable and aligned with them. This style was not often used by medical doctors, however, nor even school teams at times. It is difficult when you feel that a practitioner is talking "at" you, instead of "with" you. When you have a practitioner wanting to get to know your child and your struggles, but also importantly, wanting to learn his or her strengths and who your child truly is, it makes a world of difference. I know this is often impacted by time constraints of doctors and school teams, but a relational approach in meeting with parents does not necessarily take more time during an appointment. I found myself anxiously writing down talking points for appointments to be certain I could ask my questions, and not get flustered by the time constraints and forget what I needed to get clarity on. Sometimes I left the appointment feeling empowered, but often I was exhausted from the emotional energy I spent gearing up for the meeting and disappointed in not getting the answers I needed.

The third Principle is "recognize what you bring to the interaction." This idea became very real to me as I worked with families going through diagnosis and adjustment to disability at the same time I was going through my own adjustment process. It was very important for me to continue in my psychotherapy as a parent because I had to make sure I was aware and vigilant about boundaries and not projecting my own experience onto others. I also needed to make sure I was practicing my own self-care and honoring the experience that was separate and personal to me. In the practice of psychology, it is easier to maintain boundaries and provide appropriate insight and care to clients who hold concerns different from those you are currently dealing with in your own personal life (i.e., clients who have different diagnoses, family dynamics, etc.). For me, it was challenging that I was working in the same vein with families who at times mirrored what I was going through as a parent. I had to stay vigilant about my own personal journey and aware of what I brought into therapy sessions with families. It definitely took more care on my part to stay aware and receive my own support.

As parents go through this process, it is important to "discuss matters that go beyond your traditional role," which is the fourth Principle. Doing this is often foreign to psychologists who have been trained to maintain strict boundaries and focus on client needs and goals only within the confines of the therapy session. This varies depending on the kind of theoretical perspective they have been trained in (e.g., psychodynamic, cognitive behavioral, family systems, etc.). I often use a cognitive behavioral approach, which can be very practical in helping families solve problems and access support, and I do not hesitate to think of ways to support families outside the therapy office which can be time intensive. For example, I may help parents find an appropriate summer camp for their child with a disability, or I may help advise about how to access Social Security Disability Income (SSDI) or supportive housing for adult clients on the spectrum. There are many other examples, and parents truly appreciate additional support, particularly as they are going through the process of adjustment with their child.

The fifth Touchpoints Principle is "value passion wherever you find it." I have been continually amazed by the resilience and fighting spirit of so many parents with whom I have worked. When the intense emotion from the parents can be daunting, I find it critical to remember the stress of what they are going through based on my own experience. For example, a parent might be very angry because they cannot navigate the school system successfully to have their child tested or receive services. It can feel frustrating, disempowering, and demoralizing while they wait and watch their child continue to struggle without a plan. Working through this anger in parent sessions is really important. It can easily spur them to be proactive and vigilant, but it also can take a toll on all concerned.

"Focus on the parent-child relationship" is the sixth Principle that I continuously use in my therapy sessions because parents are the ones spending the most time with the child. The therapist really provides an outside, ancillary role to help guide and facilitate parent/child interactions. When I worked in Floortime[6] with children on the autism spectrum (Greenspan and Weider), the parents were always part of the session, playing with their child. I would coach them in different Floortime techniques. This approach empowers the parents to be responsive, following the child's rhythm and engaging with their child. Too often, parents feel isolated and helpless as they are going through the process of evaluation, diagnosis and accessing support for their child with special needs. This Principle supports the core premise that the ability to engage in many different contexts and relationships between parent and child is not only essential but also paramount to positive outcomes.

Focusing on the quality of interactions also integrated well with the seventh Touchpoints Principle, "look for opportunities to support mastery." As I played with the parent(s) and child, I would emphasize how I loved that they engaged in a certain way or

---

[6]Floortime is a therapeutic approach primarily designed for children on the autism spectrum. It includes observation, opening circles of communication, following the child's lead, extending and expanding the play and working with the child to close the circle of communication. Parents are a key component of this approach as they learn how to do Floortime at home with their child.

followed their child's lead, for example. This was critical in giving parents confidence and a sense of mastery as they were going to be their child's primary play partner. It would also bolster their energy to continue being engaged at home, in the grocery store, during play dates, etc. I remember using this approach with Caroline to help her expand her ability to play and interact, and I taught my husband as well as Caroline's babysitters how to do the same. I identified with other parents who have a child with a disability and are often told what is wrong with their child or how to parent differently. Touchpoints Principles really draw on the parents' strengths and how practitioners can help bolster their sense of efficacy with their child.

The eighth and final Principle is "value disorganization and vulnerability as an opportunity." This is a tough concept to embrace as a parent going through a difficult adjustment with their child's disability. I often find that at these moments, parents seek me out to receive support and get perspective on their situation. It is a time when practitioners may have more impact because parents may be more open and willing to hear and share ideas about their child. It is often a very raw time, and I know I experienced this with both Caroline and Jules. I did not like feeling disorganized and vulnerable around others, particularly other professionals, and I had the misconception that I needed to at least pretend to be strong and organized. The practitioner can play such an important role here as can other support people in your life, friends and family. They can be the "calm in the eye of the storm."

As a parent, I tried to be this for my family and extended family during the process with both girls, but I needed someone to be "the calm" for me, too. I often found that talking to my therapist or a friend who was in the psychology field was very helpful. I knew I needed support instead of just feeling like I could only play that role for others. Having people ask me question after question was exhausting. I did not have the answers. I really valued someone just listening and not giving me advice or guidance unless I directly asked for it. When someone asks a lot of questions, it can leave us feeling blamed or responsible for not doing enough, not trying everything possible, and it can even lead to arguing about the diagnosis. I saw this in my practice as well, particularly with extended family members rejecting the diagnosis of autism for their grandchild, for example. This can promote tension in families, friendships and social circles at a time when the parent truly needs support and acceptance.

As a psychologist, I found that working in my practice with clients helped me process all of my feelings in real time. I was walking alongside parents on different phases of their journey of adjustment. Whether it was a learning disability, autism, depression, or anxiety, they were processing how to reorganize and reorient to a new reality. When I worked with families and felt that I was making some positive impact, it helped me stay calm in my own family's adjustment process. When I came back home after seeing clients in my private practice, I felt renewed and empowered to tackle the obstacles before me with medical appointments, hearing aid fittings, evaluations, and therapy.

In summary, it is helpful to remember the Touchpoints model, as a clinician and even as a parent. More and more pediatricians and other clinicians are being trained in this model. I have noticed this with my daughters' pediatrician and others in more recent years. This can be such a difficult time as you are trying to adjust to a disability. It is really important to find the calm in your life and let others support you. These are some important points to remember:

1. Give yourself time to do self-care. Breathe, let go of some of the pain and guilt, or at least put it on hold, through spending time with family and friends who are not necessarily part of the daily painful reality. These challenges will still be there when you can come back refreshed and deal with them again. Many parents in my office voiced the concern of "taking their eye off the ball" or feeling like they cannot pause on their quest for answers or support for their child. You may feel that if you do pause, you are letting down your child or

failing as a parent in some way. Reframing this to not being neglectful, but striving for balance and self-care, is a healthy perspective. It is also incredibly important to refuel for the journey that lies ahead.

2. It is very important to have an identity outside of parenting to help balance your adjustment to disability and maintain your energy to deal with crises, continuous troubleshooting and daily challenges. This is part of self-care. It is crucial to not be exclusively tunnel-focused on what's next. It helps broaden your perspective, providing a way to step back and feel you are only looking at one part of your life.

3. If you have a husband, wife or partner, take turns! "Ham and egg it!" One person cannot carry the bulk of the burden by themselves. Your partner can give you a break. They may also show you a different way of approaching the challenges, a new perspective that might be refreshing and encouraging.

4. Set boundaries with friends and family about how you need to take breaks and not talk exclusively about the challenges in your life. It is important to protect yourself so that you don't always have to field questions from friends and family. It's okay to redirect the conversation and acknowledge that you may not have the answers they are hoping and looking for. It's important to note that questioning can be the way some people cope with their own anxiety or try to help. Many will appreciate it if you let them know what kind of support is actually most helpful to you.

Chapter 4:

❧

Here We Go Again:
Adjusting to Multiple Diagnoses

Several months after we moved to California, Caroline seemed to be settling in and hitting her stride. Her IEP continued as she started first grade, but we could already see a major difference in her being able to spend so much time outside in warm weather, swimming and doing other activities. This seemed to help her with sensory integration in a natural, outdoorsy way.

In contrast, Jules was struggling quite significantly with stomach complaints and digestion. In addition, she had to wear hearing aids to school in order to amplify sound in class, while the teacher wore a microphone to lessen the background noise of the room. This obviously proved difficult for her in trying to meet friends and read social cues, particularly in a new environment. Jules shared an essay she wrote for her college application about a distinct memory she had of this period:

"The first real memory I have of using my voice for the first time was in a classroom. I was in preschool. I had also just started wearing my new hearing aids. They were custom made for me: Light blue with sparkles, just how I wanted them. I was hardly aware of how severe my hearing loss was because my parents did a great job at making me feel positive. However, my teacher was easily annoyed by my humming in class which I often did to feel safer. My mom pulled me out of that school after I was called a "bad kid" by this teacher. I needed to use my voice and my mom did whatever she could to find a place that would allow me to do so."

I think I had temporarily blocked out this part of her story probably because it was so painful and difficult, yet it was telling that she wrote about this experience. This was a time where I had to become a fierce advocate for Jules. I have always found when I can really do something and feel that I am having some impact, I can cope with the hurdles in front of me.

This part of Jules' story, and so much of our collective experience, reminds me of Internal Family Systems Theory developed by Richard Schwartz, Ph.D. (1997). The premise is that we all have parts of ourselves that mirror what we felt like as a younger child. But these parts do not reflect the reality of who we are now in our current stage of life. These parts are stuck at the time they developed to protect us. We have grown up, but they have not. We often try to confront these difficult parts or feel ashamed of them. In this model, the parts of our psyche are: Manager, Exile, Firefighters and the Self (Schwartz, 2021). The Manager is a part that is a protector of the system and attempts to keep the person in control of every situation and relationship to protect us from feeling triggered, hurt or rejected. The Exile is a part that "holds painful emotions that have been isolated from the conscious self for protection of the system and carries burdens from being wounded. Firefighters also protect the system but act after exiles are upset to either soothe them or distract them. The Self is the core or center of the person that when differentiated acts as an active and compassionate leader." (Schwartz, 2022, p. 2)

We all have conflicting parts of ourselves that we can see at critical times such as making a big decision. When we were going through that journey with Jules, I always gravitated toward Manager and felt lost if I could not advocate, problem solve and protect her. I still find this today with other crises and hurdles we face. I feel the need to support and protect and do something to help mitigate pain and hurt. I am sure this is a major reason for my career choice. I need to care for and solve problems for others. If I can't play this role, I feel out of sync, not valued, and lost. This theory helps me understand the desire I have to fulfill this role. I do not want to avoid it or feel self-critical, but I want to be aware of it as I do not need to always play this role. There is value in being caring and compassionate without being fully the "Manager," because that role can at times thwart the development of resiliency and agency in others. This state obviously adapts to the developmental stage at which you are parenting your children. Children, particularly children with special needs and significant medical needs, need someone to manage their treatment program with their school or medical teams and advocate for them. What is difficult to recognize is when the boundary is crossed from advocate to manager and controller of all aspects of your child's life. Often, this response is based on the fear that if you let go of control, there will be more trauma and negative impact in your child's life.

❧

Jules had always seemed to have a sensitive stomach and was prone to reflux since she was a baby. We treated these symptoms while we lived in New York, but no one suggested more than a possible food allergy or reflux. With an increase in symptoms, we wondered if it was anxiety resulting from the move, but we felt puzzled. Jules had just turned four when we moved. It was not as if we pulled her out of middle school or high school with many ties and deep friendships. We knew that she missed her babysitter, Sandra, who was like a member of our family. Still, we could not see how this would make her throw up on the way to preschool, for example. It seemed like she got sick right after breakfast on most days.

Just as we had in New York, we found a gastroenterologist in the Bay Area. Shortly after the doctor gathered her history and we had several appointments with him, he recommended doing an endoscopy. We were reluctant as Jules had already had two ear surgeries with bad results. We were very paranoid that something new could go wrong. I also did not know why we would do an endoscopy or what the doctor was trying to rule out. It was very concerning, however, that Jules had started losing weight, which was a significant negative development from the doctor's perspective.. We also noticed that she was bruising easily, only had short bursts of energy but no sustained stamina, and seemed irritable at times with no apparent trigger.

Then, fortuitously, I attended a seminar hosted by a dear friend of mine, Jen, to promote awareness of celiac disease and her new gluten-free food company. I remember prior conversations with Jen about my worries regarding Jules and whether this could be a food allergy. When I was sitting at the seminar with a group of parents talking about their children with celiac disease, it clicked, and my heart sank. I came home and talked to Matt immediately about what I had heard from some of the other parents. It sounded just like what Jules was going through. Could she have celiac disease? I went back to her gastroenterologist and asked him if he was considering celiac disease for Jules. He said yes and my heart sank further. Now we were on the road to a new diagnosis, and a new set of serious health issues for our daughter.

We started by doing blood work, and her doctor said her numbers indicated she had been feeling terrible. He said, imagine if you had a bad headache and nausea every day, almost all the time. We then moved forward with the endoscopy and biopsy, which confirmed severe celiac disease. We could not believe that Jules had yet another serious medical problem to treat and cope with. At the same time, I was seven months pregnant with our youngest daughter, Abigail, and I could not fully process all we would have to do to make our house safe and gluten free for Jules. It seemed like an incredibly daunting task. We already felt emotionally depleted with the hearing loss and were still hoping for her ears to heal. I had not even begun to think how all of this would impact her life in a long-term way. I did not know how I was going to manage all of this, especially emotionally.

We felt torn because, on the one hand, we were very relieved that we had an answer for her weight loss and nausea. But, on the other hand, we were beginning to realize the seriousness of this disease and how it would impact her life. It was yet another significant "disability" for Jules, and we wished we could take it away. Caroline even commented, "Mom, I wish we could all take turns having celiac disease so Jules did not have to have this every day." We wanted to share the burden, but it just doesn't work out that way.

❧

During this time, we had major family moments to celebrate but at the same time we held so much worry for Jules. We had Caroline's triennial IEP meeting[7] and the comprehensive evaluation showed that she no longer qualified for special education services. We were thrilled with this news! We welcomed a new baby daughter, Abby. We felt overjoyed with her birth and delighted in watching Caroline and Jules be wonderful big sisters to her. I am reminded of one of the Touchpoints Parent Assumptions, which I introduced in Chapter One: "All parents have ambivalent feelings." This definitely rang true for me as I felt like we were bridging the worlds of joy and sadness. Resch and his colleagues describe caring for a child with a disability as "full of triumphs and joy as well as challenges and stress" (2018, p. 224). In our family we had both sides. I felt amazed by Jules, so proud of her resilience, and yet I was also worried about her future.

This pendulum swing of emotions can cause parents of children with disabilities to be at risk for psychosocial distress. In their study surveying parents through focus groups, Resch et al., (2018) found several themes related to parental well-being:

1. Access to information and services
2. Financial barriers to obtaining services
3. School and community inclusion
4. Family support

---

[7] A triennial evaluation occurs every 3 years with the Student Services Team. Though the team meets yearly, every 3 years, the team completes a comprehensive evaluation in all of the areas that the student receives services to determine eligibility to continue the IEP. This includes standardized testing, teacher questionnaires and observations and parent questionnaires.

All of these factors impacted us as we navigated the territory with Jules' situation. We experienced difficulty with accessing information and received conflicting information with Jules's surgeries and hearing loss, as well as her celiac disease. Do you ever feel like you spend endless time on the phone with a medical office receptionist but cannot get past them to speak to the doctor? I know I felt like I spent way too much time trying to figure out what the best course of action would be without having access to a medical doctor to talk through the decision-making process.

Financial barriers can also be overwhelming, particularly as you are working with insurance companies, and the person making the decision on coverage may not be versed on your child's disability. This obstacle can leave caregivers feeling paralyzed, exhausted and hopeless as they try to navigate the daunting world of insurance coverage, reimbursement and financial support for treatment of disabilities.

School and community inclusion is vital as well for parents of children with disabilities. We were fortunate to be in a very inclusive community in California, and the public school environment was very supportive. However, this varies tremendously in different areas of the country or even within the same town. We had to do a lot of research on the public schools and their mindset of inclusion before we were comfortable relocating our family to that community.

In addition, family support is crucial. I found that my immediate family was incredibly important to help share the burden (i.e., "see saw" with you in strength and resolve at times when you might be feeling discouraged). Also, extended family can play an important role as they are often not involved in the day-to-day routine and life with your child. They may be more objective than you can be because they are one step removed from the pain and worry. They can also provide respite for you by running errands, babysitting, or driving your child to a doctor's appointment.

Finally, emotional support is indispensable. Though not explicitly addressed in the Resch study, I want to highlight the importance of seeking support in the form of counseling and in the community. Parents need to feel that they are heard and have a space to name their feelings. Counseling can provide a safe space for individual support when parents may feel that they are supporting everyone else in the family and need to feel they are not alone. There is also a community of people who can share the burden with them, where they can connect with others who have been through some version of what they have experienced. Spending time with friends who can provide a shoulder to lean on can serve as a protective factor as well, offering protection against feeling isolated and alone in their struggles.

You may remember that I presented the Touchpoints Parent Assumptions in Chapter One. Since I am going to refer to Assumptions three through five again in this chapter, let me refresh your memory of the points:

Touchpoints Parent Assumptions

1. The parent is the expert on his/her child.

2. All parents have something critical to share at each developmental stage.

3. All parents have strengths.

4. All parents *want* to do well by their child.

5. All parents have ambivalent feelings.

6. Parenting is a process built on trial and error. (Brazelton & Sparrow, 2003)

As I felt like I was on a new journey of diagnosis with Jules and celiac disease, I leaned on these Assumptions. They also reminded me of my experience as a practitioner when I worked in a pilot preschool program for children with severe autism early in my career. The assumption that "All parents have ambivalent feelings" was a theme I felt myself as a mother and also in a very palpable way with the parents I worked with in this preschool program. Part of our multidisciplinary approach (speech, occupational therapy, a facilitated classroom, and Floortime therapy) included the parents meeting weekly with me for counseling support. It was incredibly helpful for the parents to feel like they had their own individual time in counseling. We were very aware of their feelings of grief and loss and the need for a space to talk about this. We also knew that the parents had to re-fuel to have the energy to continue throughout their day and week with their child who had a severe disability.

When I watched my Floortime sessions later on video during our group supervision, I could see how the parents looked utterly exhausted and depressed. It was difficult for them to have the energy to engage during the session because they felt depleted by caring for their child with severe autism. They needed a break and wanted someone else, perhaps an "expert", to take over. Another piece was that they seemed to feel discouraged when they realized that their child was not engaging with them but was withdrawing, and avoiding their attempts to connect. This was heartbreaking and exhausting for the caregiver to experience. We coached them in Floortime to give them skills to engage with their child outside the preschool program, which would increase the child's social skills and also empower the parents.

As I sat with parents during our counseling sessions, I could hear that they often felt like they were going through their own grief process and felt alone. It helped tremendously to have a team working with them and their entire family system. Being around other parents who were also having similar experiences was incredibly helpful, too. These families needed to feel heard and supported as they were often going through family upheaval, a grief process and adjustment to a lifelong diagnosis.

Another Touchpoint Parent Assumption is "All parents have strengths." I was continually amazed at the parents I worked with in this preschool program. They were dedicated participants in the Floortime sessions, where I coached them through various developmental levels with their child's communication, play, and engagement. I reflected back on the commitment of not just the parents but the whole family, as often we included the extended family in Floortime with their child or grandchild. I could also see parents becoming "caregivers" to other parents who were just starting their journey, trying to help them through and offer guidance or someone to talk to. It was inspiring to see them move gradually from overwhelm into being a source of strength and support for others.

Also, "All parents *want* to do well by their child" is an important Touchpoints Parent Assumption. Often during my training and before I had my own children, I asked myself "Why can't the parents just do ___?" This goes back to the ambivalent feelings that the parents often have. It was important for me to understand that parents *want* to do well by their child but often are feeling stuck. Maybe it is the grief and adjustment to the diagnosis, or perhaps they do not have enough support or energy to follow through on ideas and recommendations. They can also feel overwhelmed by all the information to sift through and by coordinating care in medical and educational systems.

The final Touchpoint Parent Assumption is: "Parenting is a process built on trial and error." It is messy. We cannot control factors in parenting our child like we can in a science experiment. We learn as we go. At the same time, we need to be careful not to let that open ways to blame ourselves. No one can predict the future or give us an accurate forecast of what lies ahead. There are many different roads we can take, different decisions along our journey. Sometimes, it is impossible to have all the information we need before making a decision, and we need to accept that we made the best decision we could with the information we did have.

In summary, it is important to give space to "the unknown" and try to get comfortable in not knowing the "right" plan or way forward in a particular moment. As I journeyed through the process of Jules' diagnosis, I wish I had a professional working with me that used the Touchpoints mindset. That would have empowered me and helped dampen some of the feelings of inadequacy I experienced as a parent. It's also important not to lose sight of the fact that you are your child's greatest asset and know your child best! Below are some helpful tips to keep in mind: .

1. It is okay to live in the ambiguity. Though it's a very uncomfortable place, it is a necessary place. Sometimes it is the only way you will arrive at a plan or a solution, at least in the short term.

2. Honor yourself as a parent who is on a journey of your own unchartered territory. You are not supposed to have all the answers. Believe it or not, the medical professionals do not have all the answers either!

3. Remember how much your children teach you about life, yourself, and being a parent. It is a rich education with many different degree paths!

4. Let go of the shoulds: "I should have known. I should have been more proactive. I should have been able to protect my child from this." It only leads to more downward spiraling and self-defeating talk. Hindsight is always 20/20. No one can see the future. We are doing the best we can as parents trying to understand our challenges and how best to advocate for our children.

Chapter 5:

Being an Advocate and Holding on to Hope

As we continued with Jules on her journey of adapting to celiac disease in her daily life, we were also grappling with what it meant for her long term. I had been reading about how children and adults with celiac disease were often, in effect, malnourished due to lack of absorption of nutrients, and after diagnosis and lifestyle changes, they experienced much more robust health. This could come in the form of weight gain, growth in height, an increased sense of well-being and positive mood, and less irritability. My husband and I both asked ourselves, if that could happen with others who were diagnosed with celiac disease, why wouldn't it happen for Jules? We took another leap and asked, "What if this could help her ears heal?" We knew that was a BIG leap.

I had become a "novice expert" in celiac disease, learning very quickly what vitamins Jules had not been absorbing, like vitamin K, vitamin D and vitamin E, which are critical for growth and healing the body. I ensured that meals I offered her were not only strictly gluten free but also rich in these vitamins and other minerals that promote growth and healing. I spent time with my friend, Jen, who had the gluten-free food business and began understanding what to look for in the store, what "gluten free" versus "certified gluten free" meant for someone who has severe celiac disease like Jules. I learned how many parts per million would qualify a food as gluten free. I also learned about the sneaky gluten that could be found in certain shampoos, toothpastes, vitamins and other products.

Over the next six months, we noticed Julianne's health drastically changing with the gluten-free diet. She gained several pounds and grew an inch. Her face filled out and she looked much healthier. We could now see just how malnourished she had been before the diagnosis. In contrast to the good news, however, the doctor commented that she had grown quickly in the past several months but her bones had not increased in density at the same rate. As a result, *she also had osteoporosis and later broke her arm in a freak accident at a swim team party. Understandably, it takes longer for bones to become dense when you are having a growth spurt. It was difficult for us to watch Jules go to school with hearing aids and a cast on her arm, but she did not miss a beat and went off every morning with a smile on her face. She also did not seem to care that she still had to wear a swim cap over and plugs in ears, as well as a protective covering over her cast when she swam. We marveled at her strength of spirit and resilience.*

At around the same time, we went back to her local ENT in Oakland for a follow up appointment. Jules had commented that her right ear felt a little strange, like there was something in her ear. During the exam, we were dumbfounded when the doctor said that the hole in her right eardrum appeared to be closing! We spoke about the celiac disease and wondered if there was a connection between the gluten-free diet and a new-found ability to absorb vitamins. Whatever the cause, it felt like the dawn of a new era because we finally had HOPE!

We returned to the ENT doctor a couple of months later to follow up, and miracle of miracles, her right eardrum had in fact closed! He cautioned us that the left eardrum may not close due to the size of the perforation in the drum (where one hole had combined with another), but he said that it looked like it might be trying to close. We were excited about this news but knew the left eardrum closing was a long shot. Several months later, however, (one year since starting on the gluten-free diet), Jules' ENT examined both eardrums. The right was still closed and intact. He checked her left ear drum and I held my breath. Jules probably was holding her breath, too. It had closed too! Jules jumped up and hugged her doctor. I laughed and cried at the same time. We could not believe it! Jules kept saying "Thank you, thank you!" and we were both completely overjoyed. I called Matt, my parents and his parents immediately to share the news. They were all completely astounded, relieved and grateful.

This time was pivotal for our family. We all felt a huge sense of relief and a strong sense of hope. I became even more of an advocate in any way that I could for Jules, and I felt incredibly fortunate that I made the connection between celiac and her eardrums not healing. The fact that Jules's eardrums had now both healed was truly a modern-day miracle. She only had twenty percent of her left eardrum intact before it healed, and we had been ready to do the tympanoplasty surgery even though it carried a decent risk of not working. Her ENT doctors both at Oakland and Stanford Children's hospitals had never seen something like this happen before.

I felt so empowered and encouraged by this healing that I had to tell people about the importance of diet and what impact it had had on Jules. I spoke to a few people whose children had just been diagnosed with celiac disease and went to the store with someone who wanted help navigating safe gluten-free foods for their child. I was appreciative of my friend, Jen, who did this for me a year ago, so I wanted to pass along the assistance to others. I became an advocate at local grocery stores when they did not carry certain brands that were certified gluten free and ordered cases of these items for them to stock. I complained about grocery items that were labeled gluten free but in fine print stated that they were made "in a facility that processes wheat." Of course, because of cross contamination, these food items would not be safe for someone who has celiac disease. Later, I decided to train as a gluten-free diet coach to help certify certain restaurants as safe for my daughter and other people with celiac disease.

As a parent, advocating for Jules helped me feel like I could do *something* to help her when I felt many things were out of my control. Being an advocate in our child's chronic disease or disability is empowering and mitigates feelings of helplessness and hopelessness. It facilitates adjustment to the disease or disability. When we can help others who are struggling and share some of our knowledge, it can refocus us outside of our own stress and struggles, and it can be gratifying to give support to another. Just like the parents I worked with at the preschool program and throughout my clinical practice, I could see the direct benefit of celiac parents helping others who were in an earlier stage in their process of adjustment. It made the parents feel like they were able to pay it forward and help support others by giving them ideas and guidance based on their own experiences. Most of all, they understood first-hand where the other parent was coming from and what the journey ahead of them might be. This is powerful for everyone involved because it offers hope.

Hope is a strong motivator that all parents need to hang on to. Dr. Mary Lamia captured it this way, "Hope structures your life in anticipation of the future and influences how you feel in the present. Similar to optimism, hope creates a positive mood about an expectation, a goal, or a future situation. Such mental time travel influences your state of mind and alters your behavior in the present". (2011, p. 1) Looking back, I felt incredibly hopeless with the additional diagnosis of celiac for Jules. I returned to all of the questions I had before, "Why Jules?" and "How did this happen?" Those questions are a normal part of the grief and adjustment process (Livneh & Antonak, 2018). But they can make you feel stuck after a while and unable to move forward.

I always listened carefully to doctors who left the door open for improvement and had a negative reaction toward doctors who just thought medically about what they believed was possible and impossible. Parents need to keep hope alive for their own day-to-day functioning. There is always a possibility for symptoms to improve, the body to heal in some way, or something surprising to happen to mitigate the disability or disease. From Snyder et al., (1991), Lamia goes on to summarize, "Hope shapes your methods of traversing your current situation. The cognitions associated with hope—how you think when you are hopeful—are pathways to desired goals and reflect a motivation to pursue goals" (p. 1).

I knew we still had a long journey ahead of us with Jules's celiac disease. I always found hard emotions resurfacing at milestones like birthdays, starting a new school year, etc. It was difficult not to feel sad that this disease was not going away. While we were thrilled she had her hearing restored and she no longer needed hearing aids or would have a lifelong disability of hearing loss, we knew she would always have to cope with celiac disease. This is all part of the process of acceptance, redefining, and reintegrating the disease or disability into your life (Livneh & Antonak, 2018). It is also the process of letting go of what could have been.

In this arena, Jules was my best teacher. She would not let celiac disease define her or hold her back. She never missed out on a birthday party, play date or travel because of her celiac disease. It required more planning and thoughtfulness on my end, such as preparing food that was similar for a birthday party or bringing her a gluten-free cupcake. Sometimes, I would prepare gluten-free food that she would take with her, for example, to her fifth grade camp due to our concern about cross contamination. I would vet hotels and restaurants when we traveled ahead of time, sometimes requiring many hours of research, phone calls and emails to ensure they would be extra careful with her food. The good news is that Jules has now been able to travel internationally, to other countries on three other continents, and for the most part, stay safe from gluten!

Naturally, Jules was angry and sad at times and would ask "Why do I have to have this . . . This is so frustrating." I knew I just had to listen to her, be empathic and not try to fix everything. As Jules grew and matured into a teenager, celiac disease became a little trickier as she wanted to eat at restaurants just like her friends. Sometimes she was able to order something safe, but other times she took risks with the staff possibly not understanding celiac disease and cross contamination. Eventually I had to let go of being able to control her diet through my cooking and food preparation. It was now time for her to learn how to advocate for herself and weigh the risks of eating out at restaurants. This was difficult for me as I wanted her to continue to stay healthy with the disease, but she has done a great job stepping into the responsibility of caring for herself.

Jules also has taken full advantage of her regaining hearing ability as she loves to sing and is now attending a conservatory studying classical voice. This has been a love of hers since we can remember and would not be part of her life if she still had hearing loss. We never thought this was possible when she was three years old and wearing hearing aids, but we stayed *hopeful* and now cannot imagine her life any other way.

Many clinicians are now adopting a more strength-based approach versus a deficit approach and encouraging hopefulness with families. Whether it is a physical, emotional or behavioral disability, there are many strengths in children and teens that can be capitalized on when the parents approach the future with this hopeful lens. In the past, medical practitioners and even psychologists were trained under the disease model and were careful to avoid giving false hopes. I have always found in my life and in my clinical practice, however, that there is no harm in being positive and hopeful with families. There should not be parameters on hope and what positive family support can do for a child. When parents feel more hopeful, they feel more empowered and are more likely to participate actively in various therapies with their child. They are more likely to advocate for their child as well. As we personally experienced, miracles can happen, as can other amazing events that you could have never predicted, e.g., a new evaluation result, or a new therapist or practitioner who can make a big difference in your child's trajectory. A new lease on life can be created, a new reality that can help you power through.

In summary, I always remind parents that they can be their child's fiercest and most powerful advocate. Don't sell short the power you have as a parent to help your child, whether it is during a medical, educational or social challenge. You know your child best! Even though everything changes so quickly with children, as a parent, you see them in so many environments and contexts. Doing something for your child even in the face of adversity and extreme challenge helps promote feelings of self-agency and hopefulness. In my many discussions with parents in my practice, the common thread for all of them is "I had to do *something*." If you are not feeling like you can have impact, the result is feeling helpless and hopeless. Some helpful tips to remember are as follows:

1. Seek out other parents who have experienced challenges with their children. There are many groups for parents of children with special needs and medical challenges. Not only will it reaffirm your shared experience but you might get very useful ideas about how to help your child, resources to tap into and sources of financial support.

2. Give yourself time. There is no timetable for helping your child. Things will unfold as new knowledge becomes available and the course of treatment becomes clearer.

3. Step away from all of it to give yourself space. You can't be helpful to your child at 3 am while you scroll through endless possibilities and fears in your mind. Take care of yourself during this process.

4. Remember that the path forward is often unclear for a while, and you can only do the best you can with the information you have.

Chapter 6:

❧

The Pandemic:
How it Impacted Families
and the Socio-Emotional Health of Kids and Teens

Lockdown: The Beginning

In late January, 2020, Caroline came home from high school and asked us about the Coronavirus. She had been learning about it in her Environmental Science class and they also just watched the movie Contagion. Matt and I assured her that this was not like that movie and probably more like bird flu was in years past. Caroline tends to be a "worrier," much like her mother! But Matt and I both felt that this was over dramatized. We spent President's weekend down in LA and we remarked how quiet it was with less tourists. The hotel manager said that many of the tourists from China canceled their travel because of the Coronavirus. Now I was starting to feel worried.

❧

Up until now, I have spoken about the adjustment process to disabilities. Now I'm discussing our experience during the pandemic. Both of these topics speak to trauma. The pandemic posed compounded difficulty to those who were already trying to help their children with disabilities. But now everyone was experiencing collective trauma. Since we all went through the pandemic at the same time, it was difficult to get support from different people in our community. Many people felt anxious and depleted and did not have the emotional wherewithal to build others up, offer hope and a different perspective like you could in an individually experienced traumatic event. This was on a massive scale and impacted everyone. We all had our own experiences, good and bad, but ultimately, many people endured trauma during this time. Whether it was losing a loved one to Covid, not being able to visit family members (particularly elders), our children no longer being able to attend school in person, missing major developmental milestones and celebrations, trying to work from home in an effective way while managing our children in online school, feeling relationships fracture due to political polarization, or losing community, it was a challenging time for everyone.

We all have a "flashbulb memory" of where we were when we heard that schools were shutting down due to the Covid pandemic. For me, it was on Friday, March 13, right before the girls' spring break. I remember reassuring my daughters that this was temporary and schools would reopen after spring break. Then I remember reassuring them that they would reopen by May 1, and then by the beginning of the next school year. We parents were completely blindsided. The whole world was blindsided. We have had other viruses in our society, like bird flu and challenging influenza seasons, but nothing like this.

Schools were scrambling to try to pivot to online instruction. The platforms that we used were challenging at best. Students had trouble connecting to Zoom, staying in the virtual waiting room and waiting to be let in. Uploading assignments on different platforms was difficult and often did not work. Doing all of this was cumbersome and inefficient and became very discouraging to students and parents alike. At our home, we spent a lot of time trying to troubleshoot problems with Wi-Fi, particularly when everyone was on a Zoom call at the same time. Trying to navigate break-out rooms and embarrassing moments with teachers and classmates hearing their home life on Zoom, siblings walking in, and not having privacy all presented as extra challenging situations. This was particularly true

50

in lower income homes where multiple family members shared one space. These families often did not have access to a private area to take an online class or focus on their classwork, much less any outside homework or projects.

In our household, I spent many hours in crisis mode, trying to troubleshoot internet issues and emailing the schools with questions. I had difficulty uploading assignments for my daughter, Abby, who was in second grade. I oftentimes could not save the assignment and would have to start all over again. I remember sitting next to Abby to watch her online class videos and try to help her get started on assignments. I felt very divided in my attention, with a sense of urgency and frustration as I knew that she would have to navigate this on her own once I stepped out of the room. When I left her room, I had to make a major shift in energy and attention so that I could see clients on telehealth. I found it incredibly difficult to pivot from helping her and troubleshooting online school to then being completely present and focused during my clients' sessions. I also remember feeling very tired while trying to conduct these sessions online.

Again, I will incorporate the Touchpoints Guiding Principles that I used at that time (and always use) in my clinical practice throughout this chapter. These principles are for *clinicians* of different disciplines to use when working with families. They help me maintain my focus in providing support in my practice and were especially important during the pandemic. As a reminder, the Principles are as follows:

Touchpoints Guiding Principles

1. Value and understand the relationship between you and the parent.

2. Use the behavior of the child as your language.

3. Recognize what you bring to the interaction.

4. Be willing to discuss matters that go beyond your traditional role.

5. Value passion wherever you find it.

6. Focus on the parent-child relationship.

7. Look for opportunity and mastery.

8. Value disorganization and vulnerability as an opportunity. (Brazelton & Sparrow, 2003)

To give you a sense for what it was like for clinicians during the pandemic, I had a couple of meetings with my pediatric seminar group during this time. This is a group of psychologists, psychiatrists, pediatricians, occupational therapists and speech and language therapists who meet periodically in the Bay Area to discuss different topics of interest, research and clinical cases. When we met online as a group, it was comforting to know that we were all going through this together. I remember another psychologist cautioning against scheduling clients without any break in between or scheduling too many clients in one day. Not surprisingly, we all commented on the cognitive strain and therapeutic difficulty involved with meeting clients online. This illustrates "Recognize what you bring to the interaction." We often felt limited and restricted in how we could help our clients, and I had to check in with myself to make sure I was not bringing the stress of managing online school at home for my kids into the session as well. This proved to be difficult.

In addition, I could sense parents' frustration with the telehealth format for therapy since it required their kids to spend even more time online, and it was often challenging to truly read how a child or teen client was feeling without face-to-face clues. With the kids I worked with, they often got bored, quiet or would just shut down … sometimes even turning off their computer in the middle of a session! As a result, I had to do a lot of guessing and making inferences with clients about their current emotional state. Often I could only see part of my clients' faces since they did not position their camera in the best way or preferred not to show their entire face. I also noticed clients got quite distracted when they were online with me and would access other apps, texts, etc., while in session. In *so many ways*, it is much more effective to be sitting with a client in person, truly being able to read how they are feeling and getting a sense of the therapeutic dynamic occurring between the two of you.

We providers all acknowledged how challenging telehealth was, and I felt very grateful to hear that I was not alone in this. Oftentimes, in my private practice office, I would play games or use toys in my session depending on the age of my client, but this was not feasible in the new telehealth format. Our pediatric study group recommended some online games to play during the session, and it was really helpful to get ideas about how to engage better with clients online using some of these games, a whiteboard and other tools. We reminded each other of the importance of self-care and taking breaks. We also reiterated that we did not need to solve everything for our clients, nor should we be able to help them as we could pre-pandemic in the traditional one-on-one, in-person modality in our offices. We were all dropped into this uncharted and confusing territory to navigate along with families, teachers and everyone else. I really appreciated the community of support with other providers.

In another clinical role, I spoke along with a multidisciplinary team to a church community about how to help parents of children with special needs cope with online school, as well as the lack of formal structure and in-person support services. I tried to help them organize the child's day the best they could without the rhythm of in-person school. During this talk, I emphasized that parents needed to lower expectations at this time, acknowledging they were trying to help their child cope with loss of structure and support. I suggested that they not try to become all things to their child: the teacher, speech and language therapist, OT, and psychologist. I reminded parents to try to stay in the role of parent the best they could while trying to facilitate their child's other services remotely.

So many parents could see their child changing, losing skills, regressing and losing ground even early on in the pandemic. They also were often juggling responsibilities with their other children who needed help with their online school. Meanwhile, most parents also had to work! They had to play so many different roles and were really stretched to the limit and feeling desperate. There was a lot of fear about how long the pandemic would last and how parents could keep going with all of these responsibilities suddenly thrust on them. "Value disorganization and vulnerability as an opportunity" is a Touchpoints principle that fits here. Parents experienced a lot of disorganization in trying to help their children and manage their lives with so many demands heaped onto them. I encouraged parents to spend time out of the house, on walks, hikes, drives, etc., and to check in with their kids emotionally. I also encouraged a Floortime approach (Greenspan & Weider, 2009) where the parent followed their child's lead without an agenda, just trying to engage with them and meet them where they were.

Ultimately, we got through those first few months. We became semi-expert at "putting out fires," and continually troubleshooting online platforms for school and work. Personally, we found ourselves trying to establish different routines, spending more time outside and taking advantage of hiking trails and nice weather, trying new family hobbies, like cooking as a family, gardening, and playing more games together. Professionally, many of us moved to different telehealth platforms that were more user-friendly. We were even able to attend school meetings online to advocate for our clients. Ultimately, it felt like we reinvented our lives. But summer was coming and we did not know what to do. How would our lives look different with kids out of online school?

Pandemic Continued

As the pandemic continued, I observed that we parents seemed to feel confused without the typical rhythms of school ending and summer beginning. Time took on a whole new dimension. Many of us felt that we lost time and could not remember what we were doing a week or two ago. Every moment melted into the next without distinction. There was also no opportunity to travel safely for fear of Covid. We were not able enroll kids in summer camps (though some existed that were outdoors and distanced), or have them participate in summer sports or jobs. It felt like more of the same. I remember picking up Abby's end-of-year academic work and artwork from the classroom. We had to pick it up in a bin. I decided to make an "open house" at home since we could not do it at school. The whole family walked around our living room and saw all of her work from the year. We were trying desperately to recreate some normalcy and celebrate the end of the school year.

Jules had an online middle school graduation for her performing arts school. It was sad she could not do this in person and have closure about middle school ending because we had all been anticipating her final concerts and other celebrations. Jules loved this school and would have been incredibly sad to say goodbye even if Covid had not ended it all prematurely. She was not able to end "the right way," but we got our close family together at our house to watch the graduation online and have a family celebration. Still, Jules probably thought it was really unfortunate to have to leave this phase of her life in such an anticlimactic, incomplete way.

At this time, we were also glued to the news to see which local area was spiking in cases, any news on schools reopening for the fall, and how other countries were faring. We were fortunate to be able to see some of our family with a lot of precautions. We arranged to stay in a pod with them instead of being around others so that we could keep everyone safe. It was difficult, because we often had to forgo seeing friends so that we could see our family safely.

In August, we were all anxiously awaiting news about whether our local schools could reopen. Our school district had online Board meetings that parents attended in record numbers. I was hoping and praying that Caroline could start her junior year, Jules could start her freshman year, and Abby could start third grade in person or at least in a hybrid[8] model. I attended several high school and elementary school district board meetings. I wrote letters to the superintendents of both school boards about the urgency of getting kids back to school and how we could accomplish this safely. I took on the role of both a psychologist and mother and presented data and reasons behind getting kids back to school.

Since we had a very large outside area on all campuses, many parents (including me) proposed having school outside. Parents even proposed raising money independently (not a school district expense) to purchase tents and other outdoor tools in order to make this happen. Since we live in California and seasons and rainfall are very predictable, we had the ability to have outdoor school without worrying about rain until November. In these school board meetings, however, it became quite clear that our districts were not ready to try this. They also admitted that their campuses were not ready to offer a safe hybrid model, which would have included taking out a certain number of desks, putting in portable air filters, and having visual cues for how to maintain six feet apart all throughout the school.

Along with many other parents, I felt frustrated that this was not completed over the summer. There would have been ample time to arrange classrooms with social distance, new modular air filter

_____

[8] A hybrid school model during the pandemic included some time at home for online school and some time at school for in person instruction. The hybrid model assigned students to different cohorts to reduce potential exposure to Covid. These cohorts (sometimes 2 or 3 different groups of students per grade depending on the class size) would be in school together and online together on particular days.

systems, and dots where students would need to stand to maintain six feet between themselves and another student. I saw other school districts around the country reopening in a hybrid model, and it became disheartening to me and many other parents who saw other kids going back to school, while our kids were stuck online with no end in sight. We could see our kids suffering and felt incredibly helpless to change the situation.

In our own family, we saw Jules struggle to start high school completely online, unable to meet anyone at this new school. She successfully auditioned online for a local East Bay choir, a saving grace allowing her to still be able to learn music and try to meet other new friends online. But that proved difficult since she was meeting people for the first time virtually rather than in person. Jules also sang online with her high school choir but again felt challenged to meet people in this format. Because some of the strongest restrictions were in place with any activity that produced aerosol exposure (like singing), Jules was in an activity that was one of the last to re-open in person. We were grateful that at least she could sing online with these choirs and eventually in person, masked and distanced, but she wasn't able to make friends or have a community like some kids involved in other activities or sports could do. When she was allowed to return to hybrid school in March, 2021, I remember Jules pleading with me to let her stay online because it was too "awkward" to make friends and go to school in person at this point. My husband and I pushed forward knowing that this would be best for her. Eventually she made a few friends before her freshman year ended.

Ultimately we were all blindsided by having to do online school for a full year. Our local schools in the San Francisco East Bay did not resume until March, 2021, exactly one year from when the pandemic started. At this point, one year later, we reopened in a hybrid model. Most schools around the country had started a hybrid model in the fall, though many had to shut back down a few times.

By the spring, many schools around the country were back full time with precautions. In our own community, private schools reopened in October when cases were down, but our public schools remained shuttered until spring.

⤫

During these months of uncertainty about when our schools would reopen, I was really worried about my girls. I was grateful that Caroline was able to continue running with her high school cross country team, the only time she really left the house and could see her peers. I was also feeling fearful for Caroline as I saw her slipping into depression. She is a very outgoing person and was feeling starved of in-person social interaction with her friends. I could see her diving deeper into social media as she observed other friends around the country being allowed to go back to school. I tried to limit her time on social media and talked with her about the connection between her mood and scrolling through Instagram. When we realized she was struggling with clinical depression, we quickly increased support for her. This is a poem that Caroline wrote in October, 2020.

> To my captor 2020
> Your porridge taste of doom
> Your bars choke me with no yellow
> My eyes burn blue with gloom
>
> But your knot will untangle me
> Smile under Bambi's glow
> The virus frown turn upside down
> To touch the rainbow snow

Jules had different struggles. In particular, she had a difficult time getting safe gluten-free food. She got sick from repeated gluten exposures because of difficulties with the food supply chain, which impacted access to gluten-free products we usually purchased in stores. At restaurants that we trusted in the past, we occasionally ordered take-out meals, but the staff often made mistakes and did not prepare the gluten-free food safely for someone who has celiac disease. All of this resulted in ongoing anxiety about food and episodes of getting physically sick.

Jules started getting very fearful about cross contamination in her food and started losing weight because she was avoiding eating.

Subsequently, we saw Abby struggle after going back to school. Her challenges were in the social realm, due in large part to not having been able to be in a school setting for a full year. She was having social drama with her peers, and it seemed like these kids had progressed in their vocabulary and behavior but in a maldeveloped, inappropriate way, along with very limited coping skills. It seemed that the kids were mimicking the language of much older teens (probably picked up via social media) without having the matching maturity that comes with direct life experience.

This is a very toxic combination for young kids, and I noticed how easily Abby's moods shifted based on FaceTiming with friends. She was ill-equipped to navigate these waters since social interaction occurred mostly online rather than via genuine face-to-face social interaction. It was easy for kids and teens to hide behind the anonymity of the computer rather than speak directly to someone in person. I watched how sensitive she was to many social situations with friends, trying to take on everyone else's problems, which left her feeling very depressed. Abby painted a picture during this time where she showed how she was truly feeling on the inside versus how she was trying to feel and appear on the outside. You can see her painting on the next page.

Ultimately, many parents, including me, felt helpless. We had to not only try to help our child navigate online school but also scramble to help them get creative with "connecting" with friends online, through FaceTime, and meeting outside at a distance. I did not want my kids to give up or retreat to their rooms on devices under the guise of truly connecting with friends, but we as parents had to work through many emotional issues during the pandemic to provide effective support for our children. This speaks to the Internal Family Systems (IFS) approach discussed earlier (Schwartz, 2021) "that identifies and addresses multiple sub-personalities or families within each person's mental system. These sub-personalities consist of wounded parts and painful emotions such as anger and shame, and parts that try to control and protect the person from the pain of the wounded parts. The sub-personalities are often in conflict with each

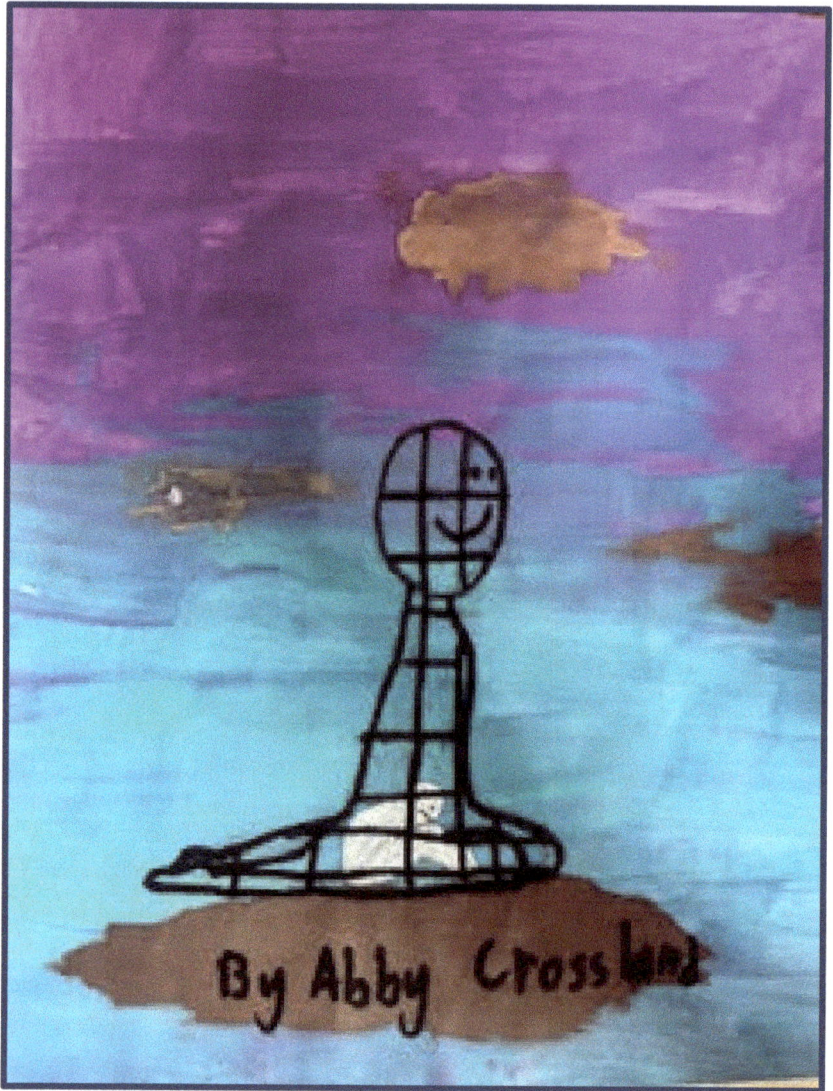

By Abby Crossland

other and with one's core Self, which is a concept that describes the confident, compassionate, whole person that is at the core of every individual"(p. 1). IFS focuses on "healing the wounded parts and restoring mental balance and harmony by changing the dynamics that create discord among the sub-personalities and the Self." (Schwartz, 2022).

According to Schwartz, the Self has many positive traits, named the eight Cs (clarity, calm, curiosity, confidence, compassion, courage, creativity, and connectedness) and the five Ps (playfulness, persistence, patience, presence, and perspective. "The presence of these traits can help identify how much of the Self is available at a given time and how much of the Self may still need to emerge." Dr. Schwartz also describes different parts of ourselves that are designed to protect us from or carry the pain of our wounds (Anderson, 2023). As mentioned in an earlier chapter, parts that are trying to protect us are called Managers, and Firefighters are parts that show up if they are triggered and want to stop the pain. Exiles are wounded or burdened parts that carry pain and trauma (Schwarz, 2023).

As parents, during the pandemic the "Manager" part was often activated to protect our kids, and we found ourselves needing to have all of the positive pieces of our Self available to our children. This came at a cost in the form of exhaustion, fear, sadness and lack of self-care. IFS would postulate that the parts of ourselves Schwartz calls Firefighter, Manager, and Exile blend at different times, particularly during stressful times, in a way that obscures our true Self (Schwartz, 2021), and what I witnessed and experienced confirms this. We found ourselves becoming hypervigilant and overreacting to perceived threats during this uncertain time. Some of these protective parts include "preventive parts" and "reactive parts" (Anderson, 2023, p. 5-6). The preventive parts include how we run our day-to-day life, being hardworking, exhausted, wanting to please, obsessing and worrying, and wanting to look good, to name a few. These can be manifested in roles like "the caretaker, the fixer, the one that understands, the one that accommodates, the one that figures things out, the fixer, and the funny one." (p. 5)

Like many mothers, I want to take care of my family, particularly my daughters, and sometimes I feel like I don't have a purpose if I can't take care of others. But we were faced with a situation during the pandemic where we couldn't fully take care of our kids because we couldn't foresee the path it would take; we were in completely uncharted territory. Many parents felt helpless all at the same time, in contrast to trauma experienced individually where others outside of the victim's own situation are available to help. The pandemic culture was different from anything we had previously been through–it was universally and simultaneously experienced.

During this time, many of us neglected our Selves to protect others, which left us feeling like we were drifting with no place to anchor. I often speak to clients about coping skills and how, before you remove a negative coping skill, you have to add a positive one: "Before you subtract, you have to add." But during the pandemic, this idea worked in reverse. So much was being subtracted in terms of lost experiences, which diluted our positive coping skills, and negative coping skills or behavior patterns were sometimes added without us being aware. In the Manager role, people protect themselves from "the outside world so that nothing triggering happens" (p. 76), but this wasn't possible during the pandemic. Self-care took a back seat to whatever triggered us, whatever "fire" we had to put out as parents.

Before the pandemic, I believe that we all underestimated the power of community and probably took it for granted. Different groups and people in our lives played important roles and shored us and our children up during stressful times. These were roles that mothers and fathers could not organically replicate because our primary role is as parents, and ultimately we care for our kids in very subjective, personal ways. Teachers, coaches, choir directors, pastors, and family friends had always been instrumental in helping our kids feel supported, not judged, and known in a different way than their parents know and love them. This support network created a balanced sense of identity for our kids in addition to what we provided them at home. But with this critical piece of support missing during the pandemic, parents felt the pressure of trying to become all of these roles to our kids.

In my family, we found that we leaned heavily on our relatives who were local. We were able to maintain a family pod during the fall that included grandparents, my brother and sister-in-law, and nieces. It was a strange time of physical boundaries with no social grace boundaries, with internalized rules such as, "if you just saw your friend, then you can't see your grandparents for fear of getting them sick." Everyone had to be an open book (or at least was expected to be one) about who they were around and where they had been, while feeling questioned intrusively about what should be private. We also, of course, felt both judgmental and judged about any lapse in protocol and "not staying safe." I have a friend who termed it "hygiene theater" because it seemed important for many of us to show how safe we were being, for example, by wearing a mask in a car when alone, wearing a mask walking outside alone, etc.

Social media had a lot of power over our teens' lives during this time since it often was one of the only social outlets. Platforms like Instagram, SnapChat, and Tik Tok were often a teen's only source of social connection. Of course, it wasn't an authentic connection but rather a way to escape and a way to compare themselves with others (i.e., who was going on a cool camping trip with their family, who was back in school, who was getting to travel somehow). Consequently, social media seemed to create much more FOMO (Fear Of Missing Out). This fear or anxiety was always in existence but became so much more powerful during the pandemic. I could see the effects of not reopening our schools in my private practice, with my friends' families and in my own family. I asserted to our local school boards that we were in a mental health crisis, as I was seeing referral after referral come my way, parents who were incredibly concerned about their kids and seeing behavior they had "never seen before." I also shared my concerns about children with special needs and learning disabilities losing precious ground, thus altering their trajectory, possibly permanently. Moreover, I was seeing my own kids struggle and felt helpless, even as a psychologist who was trained in helping clients with anxiety and depression.

To make matters worse, in our community, we saw many churches stay shuttered and remain online. Some churches did reopen, meeting outside as they could see the dire need to provide emotional and spiritual support to their congregation and community by holding services or meeting in small groups. Ultimately, some churches reopened, but many of us felt like part of our faith-based family was missing. We could no longer come together and worship with our community. This seemed to change many teens' faith journeys, too. Pastors have noted that there has been a huge decline in high-school-age teens being involved in church youth groups since the pandemic.

In summary, I discussed the pandemic in this chapter, including how we responded, the isolation and lost moments we grieved, and the academic and social development opportunities our children missed. In contrast, I mentioned there were positives that came out of this time too, such as increased time with our family, getting out in nature, game nights, cooking together, more down time together at home, and being available to meet online with clients, among others. Since the chapter looked back in time to chronicle the emotional and social ramifications of the pandemic, I have summarized a few major points below. In the next chapter, I will discuss the post-pandemic fall out, what our challenges are as we try to chart a path forward, and what you can do to help your children through this transitional time.

> 1. Recognize that you may have gone through a kind of trauma as a parent watching your child struggle. So many parents felt helpless, as though they could not have a positive impact on their child's emotional well-being. Moreover, when you saw that your child had important opportunities taken from him or her, you may have been much more lenient on them and compensated for them. You may have felt abandoned by the schools and community while your kids struggled and felt like you were the only person who "had their back."

2. Don't expect to have all the answers as a parent. We often say to ourselves: "If only I ..." or "I should've . . ." This self-talk only puts us in a negative spiral. We need to remember that this was an unprecedented and traumatic time for so many of us. We have never weathered a storm like this as parents and we were up against so many obstacles and new challenges (like increased exposure to social media, isolation, lack of community support). Give yourself some slack!

3. Understand that the aftermath of the pandemic is still unfolding. We are noticing societal shifts, and the most impacted group will likely be kids and teens who were at vulnerable times in their social, emotional and academic development. But we are unique individuals with different perspectives, and not everyone had difficult struggles during this time, with some even thriving in the more cloistered environment. The one thing we may share across the board, however, is that we have all learned a lot through this unprecedented, unexpected experience.

Chapter Seven:

Post-Pandemic Fall Out

As Caroline was leaving for college in August, 2022, she was excited, but she also carried some heaviness and anxiety about starting school. She talked about a lot of "what ifs." What if schools shut down again? What if there is another pandemic? If people did not think this was possible, how do we know it won't happen again? At that time, we weren't sure what the restrictions would be at her college. Matt and I tried to remain optimistic about college being "normal" for her. But we had not fully appreciated how far behind so many teens had fallen in their social/emotional development, coping skills, and maturity. They lost a critical time of psychological development and socialization with their peers.

This chapter will look at the fallout many of us have felt post-pandemic, and I will discuss this through the lenses of both my personal and professional life. I think it's very important to talk about the aftereffects because they are still reverberating even as this book is going to press five years after Covid began. I have had many conversations with friends and acquaintances with a common theme that "the pandemic doesn't really seem to be over." Of course it is technically over, even though some people still get Covid and quarantine, but there is no lock down of communities or schools, and many organizations do not even have guidelines or protocols in place anymore. Many people just assume that they have a cold when they get sick and will not test or do anything different with their routines. But these parents are articulating something very real: the fallout from the pandemic is still happening. We can see it in our teens and young adults, even elementary-school-age children. More studies are beginning to be conducted about this. What happened to these kids and teens when they were taken out of their social environment for over a year? How did that impact their social and emotional functioning? In some cases, there was a huge impact on younger kids and a loss of learning that will be difficult to recapture. These parents can see it but are feeling that few people are *really* recognizing it as continued fallout. Some researchers are referring to it as an "ambiguous loss" (Pauline Boss, 1999) since it isn't as clearly defined as grieving the loss of a person (though people have grieved losing loved ones during Covid) or the loss of a job or other relationship. It is the loss of a sense of security and fear that this could happen again. It is the loss of time, including events and milestones. But ultimately, this loss represents a change in how we view the world, an acute awareness that everything can be taken away from us so quickly.

Our younger kids missed out on critical time for socialization. When they returned to school, they struggled with how to socialize, interact, and problem solve through social situations. Schools observed that kids had very different behavior now out on the playground, using more adult language, inappropriate behavior, over dramatized reactions, and referencing more online experiences, such as Tik Tok, YouTube, etc. They had become more reliant on technology during the year of being out of school to make social connections with their friends, entertain themselves, and interact with online platforms for school. There was no choice but to use technology more than they ever had. But they were not mature enough to handle most of what was thrown at them or what they were exposed to. Even parents with the best intentions who monitored technology use could not completely manage this on a moment-to-moment basis due to all of their other demands, including working from home. Often the primary social outlet was the one dimensional nature of FaceTime with friends instead of the real, in-person interactions that build social skills, problem-solving and coping skills *for life*.

In both the school and work environments, the pandemic has impacted people's interest in and motivation for being around others. Some people have disengaged, remained isolated, and refused to come to work in person. Many young adults are opting to work from home and not have the in-person camaraderie and intellectual stimulation that results from coming to a workplace, having a cohort to interact with, and bouncing ideas off another person. This is vastly different from working remotely. For children, learning and social development may be derailed for a long time for those who were young during the pandemic. The impact of this time of lost structured learning, social/emotional development, and community is still unfolding for everyone, in particular teens and young adults. All of this has greatly impacted our world, economy, and socialization. There have been some positives for people not having to endure terrible commutes to work, parents being more mindful about not sending their kids to school when sick and schools being more flexible about illness and absence. But there is ongoing unease about the world being "different," "unsafe," "forever changed." It seems there is less trust in what we thought we could always count on, and how life would unfold.

Many kids, teens and young adults seem to be about a year and a half behind socially and emotionally. I have heard from many parents (friends in my community and parents of clients) that their kids truly struggled more than expected after a big life transition, like leaving for college or graduating high school. They do not seem as "equipped" to deal with being away from home. And after the pandemic ended, it was still happening. We may have had a false sense of security thinking the pandemic was "over", but it doesn't seem to be in terms of trauma and stress for this cohort of teens. It is unrealistic for us to think that taking a year away from kids and teens, who are developing social and emotional coping skills necessary to take the next step, would not have an impact.

Teenagers, particularly those who had some pre-existing anxiety prior to the pandemic, are very vulnerable to worrying about what's next. Adults often reassured them at the beginning that Covid was a passing thing, like other previous scares, which proved to be false. No one could have fully anticipated this event, and yet their trauma reaction makes it harder for teens to trust what adults say and be optimistic.

Parenting today looks different too. A recent report from the US Surgeon General, entitled, "Parents Under Pressure" warns that we are currently in a mental health crisis for parents (Murthy, 2024). This report indicated that 48% of parents are completely overwhelmed and often cannot function. In addition, 65% of parents reported loneliness. We have lost our "villages." Now more than ever, parents need community and support. They referenced the "culture of comparison" through social media where parents may perceive that they are not doing enough with their kids, not giving them enough experiences and enriched activities. We are judging ourselves severely and feeling like we are falling short. The report underscores the fact that we have to address parent mental health as that impacts kids' mental health, as well. Ultimately, parents of children and teens may feel less competent to support their kids through crises since the pandemic took so much away.

We also had to experience "re-entry" into social life and community experiences. I have noticed that I have taken stock about my priorities and gotten clearer about how I want to spend my time. Some of this is the natural aging process and reflecting on my own personal journey. But I think many of us discovered what was really important during the pandemic when we lost so much. Many people felt palpable grief regarding missing out on milestones such as graduations, birthdays and weddings. People grieved that they were not able to be with their loved ones in the hospital, visit elderly family in a nursing home, and even properly say goodbye to those they lost.

We are at an inflection point now where our communities have to redefine themselves. There has been a lot of shuffling around to different groups, affiliations, churches and friendships. In some cases, the pendulum may have swung too far in the opposite direction as parents may feel desperate to take advantage of every opportunity for their kids because of what they lost, unconsciously choosing more extracurricular activities for their kids over more relational activities for the family. We also seem to have lost some comfort in social situations, including the ability to go deep in our relationships, because of the lack of socialization during the pandemic. It may be easier to cheer for your child on a soccer field than to go to a church or spend time with a group of friends. We may feel less at ease with these more personal interactions than we used to. It is important to name what we have all been through. Current researchers call it "a shared traumatic reality" (Anderson, 2023). In addition to the trauma experienced by parents and children, psychologists have been through a lot in trying to provide care for our clients while trying to care for ourselves, and the same is true for teachers too, trying to support students as well as themselves.

Pandemic Perspectives

To gain a better understanding of the Covid aftermath, I interviewed several people in our community who had direct interaction with kids and teens during and after the pandemic. This includes a kindergarten teacher, a clinical psychologist, a high school basketball coach, a high school cross country coach and a pastor. In the next chapter, I share my interview with a school director who is also a psychologist as well as a parent interview. I interviewed them because it broadens the perspective of people's experiences during and after the pandemic. I am hoping seeing these summaries will assuage some feelings of isolation that you may have felt as a parent during this time.

In my interview with a kindergarten teacher in our community, she discussed her experience of online school, as well as the challenges and aftereffects for children as they returned to school. She reported that during the remainder of the 2020 school year, she recorded most of the lessons and provided a packet of materials each week for the students. For the 2020-2021 school year, she transitioned to Zoom and got creative by setting up a "studio" where she could teach and view her students while teaching. She had the benefit of a large screen where she could see all students. Then she provided packets, which were returned a week later as before. The biggest concern she voiced was whether the students were actually learning because it was a challenge to monitor progress. Additionally, she was concerned about access to learning as parents at home were often having to work and could not closely monitor their children. For her kindergarteners, the teacher's biggest concern was socialization. Once they returned to in-person school, she noticed that the students did not know how to "play together", and she and other teachers had to teach more social skills, like turn taking, sharing, and coping skills such as flexibility and patience. One positive the teacher noted was learning about some supplemental tools to help with the socialization piece. A curriculum program her school used and continues to use to support students' social and emotional needs was: We Thinkers Book Series (Hendrix et al., 2013). It provided students with tools to help problem solve, engage and relate to peers and staff, and they continue to use it today.

I also interviewed a clinical psychologist in our community who works with kids and teens. He discussed how he pivoted to online therapy, the challenges he experienced during the pandemic and the fall-out he notices today. Initially he felt concerned that going to online therapy could negatively impact his practice. Several of his clients terminated once the initial restrictions of doing in-person therapy began. Then he realized that he (and his wife who is also a psychologist) could do telehealth fairly easily. They recognized that they had a space at their home to do this and with no small children at home, it was fairly easy to manage. He noted that very quickly their caseloads grew, and he noticed that other practitioners were "full" and had very limited time to take on new clients. The psychologist described, however, that something was lost with certain clients when seeing them online, particularly for children with ADHD. He noted that the computer was simply too distracting for therapy to be effective. Another challenge was doing family meetings online. When a teen and parent were in high conflict, it was physically challenging for them to squeeze in next to each other to be on a single screen, and it often proved to be tense and ineffective. He then tried to troubleshoot and have the parent and teen on separate computers, but the slight lag in hearing each other led them to talk over each other and undermined the work. This experience has caused him to conclude that it is not helpful to conduct highly conflicted sessions online.

In contrast, some aspects of telehealth for the psychologist were "positive and freeing." There was greater privacy for clients at home and more flexibility in timing sessions than when they had to come to the office. Also, in the past, when clients moved out of state, he would have to terminate, but many states allowed interstate practice during the pandemic. Another positive was that with some clients, he would screen share and do things like job searching or reviewing school reports online, and that was helpful. He was able to see parents who he rarely saw in person, and they could join their child or teen during sessions that were held during the workday. This ended up being the busiest time of his career.

In addition, the psychologist works a lot with teens and young adults with autism spectrum disorder and anxiety. He stated that "many of the clients felt fine with the pandemic restrictions and preferred online schooling to busy, overstimulating school classrooms." In fact, one of his more self-aware clients remarked, "Social distancing? I've been doing that my whole life." In these cases, the clients felt like they adapted well to the structured learning and greater time offered by online classes.

In contrast, for the more socially engaged kids, he reported that the lock down seemed to be very challenging. He described having "a client who started at a large public high school in the fall of 2020 after having been in private schools to that point. It was exceptionally difficult for them to make friends, and they struggled greatly with their mood during that year and the start of the next." The psychologist stated that he has observed many of his clients adopt a "position of social isolation and avoidance and are making few efforts to overcome them now." He commented, "I think people often try to paint the pandemic as if it had one effect on people, though in my experience it was really about the interaction of social distancing with the person's pre-existing personality and coping style."

The psychologist felt that returning to in-person classes was a great thing for some clients and really challenging for others. Many of the psychologist's clients who have autism spectrum disorder (ASD) continue to struggle with the social isolation and increased depression that started in the pandemic and actually worsened with the return to in-person classes. Many of these kids got used to the independence they experienced with online school, and having to go to school and sit in class all day has been difficult. In addition, many with sensory issues had a much more difficult time adjusting when they were faced with the noise and chaos of a large school after a year of isolation.

With younger children, the psychologist reported that it is somewhat harder to determine the exact effects, but he continues to see academic delays currently that could be related to the pandemic. In his psychological testing, it is often hard to differentiate between children with some sort of underlying processing difference and those who missed pre-kindergarten and kindergarten because of the pandemic.

I interviewed a local high school basketball coach who discussed differences in student athletes pre- and post-Covid and the challenges he faces today in coaching. He did not have any interaction with the student athletes between March 2020 and February 2021 and noted that they seemed very happy to be back in person in early 2021. Since the pandemic ended, however, he noticed the student athletes seemed to be less respectful of their teammates, coaches, officials, and administration. He also described less resilience in the student athletes, for example, less ability to distinguish between pain and injury, and more fear about physical injury. The coach described that these athletes also seemed to have "more fear of failure, less mental fortitude, inability to 'flush it', and were more likely to dwell on making a mistake or disappointment rather than enjoy a success." Thirdly, the coach observed that the student athletes and parents were "more likely to blame someone else for their failure" and had "more excuses for why they didn't achieve success." Parents were also likely to place blame on the coaches rather than hold their student athlete accountable and in general seemed more anxious about their child's opportunity for success than prior to the pandemic. The coach observed that because many parents felt that their child missed out on so many opportunities and experiences during the pandemic, they may have been more permissive and lenient with other responsibilities (such as academic demands).

The basketball coach stated that he noticed a difference in the student athletes' social and coping skills. He reported that they seemed a "little less comfortable with in-person communication and more comfortable with texting and technology. For example, rather than verbally share something funny, or make a humorous remark, they would send their teammate a funny video and laugh together." He noted that team meetings were shorter because of decreased attention spans and listening skills. He also noticed that it was difficult to get the players to speak in front of their teammates when the group was together, and they were reluctant to give each other feedback during team meetings.

In contrast, a local high school cross country coach discussed the student athletes' resilience and camaraderie during the pandemic in my interview with him. I have wondered if his perspective is different from the high school basketball coach since his team was able to continue to practice with precautions during the pandemic. He noted that their resilience was very surprising and thankfully, he had the support of the athletic director at the high school to continue the running program. Since the athletes who came to practice were at low risk, they embraced the opportunity to be around others and run. Unfortunately, he explained, there was some "community policing" with adults in the neighborhoods where they were running taking pictures of them (even though they were running in pods, with precautions and with the permission of the athletic director). Sometimes runners were yelled at and heckled by adults in the neighborhoods. The coaches reassured the concerned people that the students were being safe and following protocols, but having the adults projecting fear onto the athletes took a toll, and they had to weather this stress in addition to everything else. Because of the loss of their community and social interaction, he was most concerned about the athletes who were not allowed to attend practice. He did not see some of these athletes until the fall of 2021. In summary, the coach stated that these athletes did a very good job thinking for themselves and tried to stay objective in their decision making during the pandemic. Ultimately, they really benefited from attending practice and being around others.

When I interviewed a pastor in our community, he described how challenging it was to start at a new church during the pandemic. It made it hard for him to get to know his congregants and minister to them. The church started with recordings of the service posted online at the time of the church service on Sunday mornings. Then, the church moved to outdoor services with distancing, and finally, they moved indoors with masks and distancing. He noted that both fear and uncertainty were driving motivators in our community. Often people did not know how to respond, so they responded with anger. The pastor noted that there was a fairly large group watching the online recordings and then live streaming once they moved to outdoor services and later indoor services. It was a benefit that people from across the country could tune into services and still do.

He recalled hearing from teens and families during this time about their anxiety, depression, and social isolation. He remembered speaking to parents of younger children who worried about their children's socialization and social/developmental growth as they were trying to learn these skills while everyone was masked. The pastor discussed feeling exhausted on his end, as he was trying to play multiple roles to his congregants. Now, after the pandemic, the pastor noted a difference in people. There seems to be more of a "resistance to commitment" than there used to be in the church community. He stated "as commitments to extracurricular programs accelerated, our commitment to relationships decelerated." He quoted the late Ernest Becker, Pulitzer Prize winning author, "[Death] is the rumble of panic that is underneath everything" (1975, p. 353). The pastor's point is that the ground is still shifting, unsettled and unreliable even five years after the pandemic began. In addition, we are more polarized in our political views, which contributes to relational difficulties: "It is hard to regulate and to live centered and in peacefulness."

Reflecting on the interviews of various professionals in the community who were interacting directly with kids and teens in some format, I found some key points. The teacher, psychologist and school director (whose interview is in the following chapter) all spoke about having to adapt quickly, get creative using different tools and try to make the most out of being online. I believe that most people tried their best and moved their feet quickly to help kids and teens during this unprecedented time. The basketball and cross country coaches had very different experiences. Perhaps this is due to the ability of the cross country team to continue to practice throughout Covid with an extended season. Running continued not only through the fall but also into the winter and spring as a hybrid cross country/track practice. The cross country coach discussed how it was important that he could see the athletes almost the entire time during the pandemic and was able to provide support to all of them as a coach and mentor. In contrast, basketball was only played during the winter season and they had more restrictions due to the nature of the sport. The basketball coach was not able to spend time with the athletes over a greater period of time during the pandemic to provide continuous support and mentorship. The pastor commented on the difficulty of creating community in his new church that unfortunately happened to begin during the pandemic. It was a challenge to provide support to his congregants as they were not able to meet in person. He also reflected on the post-pandemic reality which includes a "resistance to commitment" and difficulty coming together as a community instead of staying polarized.

In summary, we all were profoundly impacted by the pandemic and shared it together. The interview perspectives in this chapter depict how varied our experiences were at this time. Some of the experiences cluster for people who collectively experienced a loss, such as not being able to celebrate and commemorate important milestones (e.g., a child's high school graduation, having to cancel or postpone a wedding, etc.) . Others had the concern about loss of academic skills and social emotional skills with a younger child or a child with a disability. Regardless, we all need to re-center our lives after the pandemic. Here are some suggestions.

1. Take a break from technology and spend time directly engaging with your child or teen. It could be going for a walk or a hike or to a favorite ice cream shop. Try to meet them where they are emotionally and not have an agenda. Getting your child/teen out of the house and away from all of the distractions, particularly social media, is very healthy. Listen for opportunities to add support into your child's life. This may come in the form of counseling, or spending time with a pastor, youth director, coach or mentor. Sometimes extended family can provide critical support to your child and be a sounding board for them.

2. Listen to your body and nurture it. We often neglected ourselves during the pandemic and continue to do this in the aftermath. Self-care is so important as it will free up energy to be present and engaged with your children and their challenges, as well as yours!

3. It is important to find the balance now with advocating for and supporting your child and helping them take appropriate responsibility. It has been over five years since the pandemic started, and there is still fallout for many kids, teens and young adults. We are still learning about and seeing the aftershocks of the pandemic. Try to stay aware of the lens you may look through now and provide your child with the appropriate amount of scaffolding[9], or support, while also encouraging their independence and self-efficacy.

4. Find your community. As the US Surgeon General reported, parents are feeling significant amounts of stress and increased isolation, often leaving them feeling anxious and depressed. It is important for us to reform our villages and find emotional support, bounce ideas off of each other as parents, and support each other's families.

---

[9] Scaffolding is a technique that provides temporary support to help a learner achieve a goal that they would not be able to accomplish on their own.

Chapter Eight:

❧

Building Resilience
in Your Child and Yourself

In 2023, I attended a graduation ceremony for a school called Orion Academy. Orion Academy is a private high school in the Bay Area for teens who are "neurodivergent" and often on the autism spectrum. This school does a beautiful job of helping the senior class through a "college and transitions" class to help them get ready for being out of the house, starting a job/internship or career, going to a four-year college, community college and other options. I was incredibly moved by all the graduates' speeches they made during the ceremony. Many of them talked about this school being their "family" and giving them confidence to go on and pursue the next thing. One graduate astutely said, "I am still waiting on my manual for how to become an adult. But then I realized they are still trying to translate this from ancient times." This was such a poignant way to capture their fears, how they have had to use many strategies to get through life thus far, and how there is no clear method for tackling this next stage of becoming an adult.

I watched how the parents responded, seeing their children receive awards, give personal speeches, and receive their coveted diplomas. Most of the graduates talked about their hardships in life, getting bullied in other schools, experiencing poor mental health, feeling isolated in general and even more isolated during the pandemic. They all stood before a hotel ballroom full of other students, parents, family, friends, teachers and alumni beaming and proud that they had made it! They had gotten through a difficult time with the wonderful support of their family and this unique school program, and for the most part, they felt ready for what comes next. This shows true resilience, and the graduates seemed to know how far they had come. They described their deficits without shame or trying to craft it into a more socially acceptable kind of deficit. They knew they have a lot more room to grow and that they will have more struggles.

I am excited to see where life leads these graduates. They seemed insightful and ready to face their next challenge. I could see that they have leaned on their friends and family who truly "know" and "see" them. The insight they had about their vulnerabilities and challenges is profound and unique for any teenager, and it is an important lesson for all of us. Being around people who believe in you and build you up is vitally important. I could observe that these amazing young adults felt supported by their family and friends and their very important "school family." And the parents in attendance beamed at the resilience of their kids. They had walked alongside their children and advocated in every way for them, and it was their proudest moment to see that their children had accomplished so much and were able to look forward to the next step with pride and dignity. We can take a chapter out of their book and apply it to so many other challenges that parents face.

I interviewed Dr. Kathryn Stewart, who is a clinical psychologist and the director and founder of Orion Academy, to see how her students fared during and after the pandemic. She said unequivocally they were all negatively impacted by the pandemic and being online. However, she observed that they came back with a new perspective that being alone is not "better." Often with this population, there is a belief that, "if people would leave me alone, I would be fine." These kids and teens are vulnerable to anxiety and depression, and once you take away the community for support and socialization, the risk for psychological disorders becomes greater. The students returned to school with new appreciation for what they could do best as an individual versus in a group. The pandemic brought to the forefront how important the Orion community was to its students, and how they missed that small, tight-knit community. They realized that life becomes less socially challenging when they are on their own away from the group milieu, yet it becomes more difficult in so many other ways. Some of the students believed they had made friends online but found those friendships did not offer all of the benefits of in-person relationships. Dr. Stewart discussed counseling students to address their fears regarding socializing and taking a risk, and then helping them through the resulting process. She would tell students that we have to *try* things to know if we do or don't like them, or if we're just afraid. In general, children and teens on the autism spectrum are not risk takers, and they need someone and often a community to push them out of their comfort zone. After returning to school, they could now see that Orion offered them just such a supportive community.

I also interviewed a parent in our community who has two school age children. She described some positive outcomes of the pandemic, such as building cooperation within the family, having more time together, and doing creative projects. She mentioned that they have had to consider what they want to see in their new environment and also to be intentional and not take anything for granted. She further discussed that it is beneficial to go through hard times and see that you can get through it, and to remember that "you don't always get a practice run in life."

She commented that her kids have learned to deal with things more independently, have become more tech savvy and are better critical thinkers, even though some of the simplicity of life has been lost. She noted that the pandemic has forced parents to pay attention to technology and refocus on the basics of the human experience, and that kids in this pandemic generation will be forever changed by their experience, hopefully having realized what is truly important.

Researchers have noted that there are similarities between experiencing a traumatic event such as the pandemic and adjusting to and coping with a chronic illness (Livneh and Atonak, 2018). We go through a grief and readjustment process in both, re-consolidating a sense of self and a new world view. Cleave (2010) described enduring chronic illness in this way: "I ask you right here to please agree with me that a scar is never ugly. That is what the scar makers want us to think. But you and I, we must make an agreement to defy them. We must see all scars as beauty. Okay? This will be our secret. Because take it from me, a scar does not form on the dying. A scar means, I survived" (pp. 8-9).

We all carry "scars" from the pandemic. Whether it was from the trauma of our struggles or our kids' struggles, we are forever changed. But, we also *survived*. Some parents I have spoken to in my private practice describe feeling a new strength and resilience. Being in the trenches with their kids and experiencing those feelings of helplessness is something they won't forget. But, they feel like they have gotten through it and have a new life perspective.

People are talking about finding a new sense of what is important in their lives. What is important to you? For me, I have found that I want more simplicity in my life and more community support around me. Some activities promote needless busyness, and I can prune those out of my life. Similarly, I have spoken with many parents who have opted out of the "hamster wheeling" that can happen as we as parents with busy schedules pursue equally busy schedules for our children.

Madeline Levine, psychologist and author, illuminates this concept in her book, *The Price of Privilege* (2006). She asks why are we overscheduling and creating so much unnecessary pressure for our kids, whether it is in sports, academics, or other arenas where kids and teens already are pressured to achieve the impossible? As a psychologist, I agree that we do this at great cost. In addition, when we manufacture our children's lives and schedules, and we solve problems that are developmentally appropriate for them to solve, our children lose out on their own autonomy and sense of self-efficacy (Levine, 2006). This phenomenon is illustrated in the documentary, *The Race to Nowhere*, which highlights the heartbreaking stories of students who have been pushed to the brink, incredibly stressed out to the point of cheating for their grades and worse. They are disengaged, burned out and developing stress-related illnesses and suicidal ideation. This leads to young people arriving at college and the workplace very anxious, unprepared and uninspired (Abeles & Congdon, 2010). In my observation, the pandemic may have helped shift some of this cultural craziness. Many parents may have decided to pare back on the number of sports they sign their kids up for and instead are looking for more community-building experiences, such as through church or their neighborhood. I have witnessed parents, often with school wellness support, becoming more attuned to their child's emotional functioning and ensuring their child has more balance in their life.

We have also become more aware of the impact of isolation as new research is coming out about the importance of community for mental health, productivity and resilience. Community support is a protective factor that can help buffer stress and build coping and problem solving skills. Personally, I find myself looking for opportunities for community in any way I can find it, through my family, friends, church, and profession. I find that I feel at my best and happiest when I can be around others, interacting and contributing. More than ever, we all realize how important family is and how everything can change so quickly. I have spoken to many parents who feel grateful for what they have and try to recognize and appreciate opportunities to spend time and savor special moments with family and friends. A supportive community is of critical importance, especially with certain populations. For individuals on the autism spectrum, it can help propel them forward with new challenges, positive risk-taking, and more independence and autonomy.

Isolation from others may be a "comfort zone" for certain people, as with some on the autism spectrum, but staying in this comfort zone and avoiding being challenged by interacting with others, bouncing ideas off each other, and sharing ideas for problem solving only perpetuates the inertia, as Dr. Kathryn Stewart discussed. Even substituting Zoom meetings and telehealth for in-person meetings, although more convenient and often less challenging logistically, leaves us less connected. I've heard from a lot of friends and colleagues that they've had to relearn how to interact again in social settings. It has been awkward for many of us. But imagine if you decided to stop interacting with others. That would create inertia and make it that much more difficult to socialize and interact as time goes on.

Post-pandemic, we are more tuned into mental health in the school setting as well. Schools around the country have improved their wellness centers, adding more programs and more ways to identify at-risk kids and teens who may need psychological support. There are many parenting seminars being taught in school districts to help parents identify whether their child may need professional intervention and to offer guidance about how to support them at home. The teacher I interviewed in a previous chapter discussed how they have adopted a book series to help kindergarten students learn new coping strategies to support their social and emotional wellness. There is also greater access to online support and tools for kids who are behind in academic subjects. All of these efforts take many forms in different age groups in the school and college settings. In addition, I have observed that many college wellness programs have become more robust, with more counselors and programs being offered to students.

Regarding the advantages of technology, many psychologists now offer a telehealth option, and there is greater access to therapy since the pandemic. For many adults, having to battle traffic to get a session after work is not feasible. It is much easier logistically to fit therapy into their lives if they can have a session while in a private room during the work day. Personally, I continue to offer telehealth when I need to do an initial parent interview, parent coaching or feedback. However, I do not offer telehealth anymore as I did during the pandemic for kids, teens and young adults, as I feel that something gets lost in this format versus in person. There are occasions where I will do this temporarily when clients are starting college out of state, but I find it is not nearly as effective as in-person therapy.

Technology has helped and also complicated things post-pandemic. We often feel like we need to schedule every minute, maximize every moment with work or other commitments. In some ways, technology has made it busier for many of us as we say "yes" to more Zoom meetings, for example. I wonder if because people lost so much during the pandemic, they are now in hyperdrive trying to squeeze everything in and overschedule even more than before, perhaps to make up for lost time. More offerings are readily available due to increased applications of technology, as well.

As the parent I interviewed in a previous chapter discussed, our kids have also become more savvy using technology. This is both positive and negative. Kids can access inappropriate sites and work around different age restrictions, and it is very difficult for parents to monitor everything that their children are looking at online. Even if they try to be vigilant in monitoring their online time, many kids have figured out how to hide some of their online presence on certain sites.

On the positive side, kids can also use FaceTime to spend time with friends when they are not able to get together in person. They are experienced in accessing academic websites and tools utilized at school, which in turn will help them as they progress further in school and college. Learning different ways to search online for research purposes will help them dive deep into content for writing assignments and discern what is an appropriate source since now utilizing a "primary source" is not as available or common.

In summary, the pandemic was experienced uniquely by each individual, and it represented a watershed moment in our society as a whole. Along with the negatives, there were many positives that continue to affect us as we move forward. This has been a time to build resilience in our children and within our families, push the "reset" button about our priorities, and stay more vigilant about mental health and wellness. I think we have grown in many ways through this shared traumatic experience.

Some helpful tips going forward include the following:

1. Don't be afraid to reach out to others to broaden your community. There are lower incidences of depression in those who have community versus those who are isolated. Utilizing this support does not mean you are weak, but rather creates *interdependence* and makes you stronger.

2. Take advantage of parent talks in your community, particularly talks about tuning into our kids and teens in this post pandemic era. Pediatricians, psychologists and other professionals who work directly with kids are frequently offering these talks. They are noticing major changes in social and emotional development post-pandemic. It could be quite empowering to hear these perspectives and experience the community of parents around you!

3. Remember the importance of simplicity and encourage in-person interaction and socialization experiences with your kids.

4. Remember that everyone had different experiences during the pandemic. Mostly I find that parents of teens and young adults had an especially difficult time if it was during a milestone or big transition (e.g., starting high school or college). Other very young age groups struggled too, especially with the lack of in-person instruction and socialization, and many still need remedial help in these areas. Your experience is personal to you and is *your* narrative.

5. Think about how to "serve" others around you. Getting outside of your challenges and helping others builds a sense of self-efficacy and hope. If you stay in your own woundedness, you can get stuck, unable to

help others and challenge yourself in new ways (Tim Keller, 2011).

6. Take a break and practice self-care so that you have energy for others.

Chapter Nine:

❧

Coda

As I was writing this book, I was blindsided by another crisis. My husband, Matt, was diagnosed with breast cancer in August, 2023. This was completely unexpected and very stressful. Just when I thought things had calmed down, another wave hit. This diagnosis was traumatic for our girls and our marriage. I found myself asking, "Why didn't I insist that he get a second opinion and move forward instead of 'watching and waiting' as his doctor recommended?" Luckily, Matt ended up getting several second opinions about the treatment plan from some of the best cancer centers in the country, and we got through two surgeries and radiation. At this point, he is "clear" and is now being monitored at UCSF by one of the best oncologists in this field. I had to urge him to change treatment teams in order to be monitored in this way, but I now feel he is being treated and watched carefully by the best team possible. After advocating for my girls so many times and in so many ways over the years, this time, I had to advocate for Matt. I find myself feeling useless if I can't use that part of myself when there is a crisis going on. Ironically, I did my dissertation on women with breast cancer. During my postdoctoral fellowship, when I was training in several different pediatric clinics, Matt asked me if I thought I was being trained for something I would experience later in life with our kids. Now I can see that many of the things I was trained in helped prepare me for all the challenges my family has experienced. However, nothing can really prepare us emotionally for the onslaught of a new, unexpected crisis with those we love.

❧

We have to remind ourselves that crises and difficult moments, the waves, will keep coming. But, we can learn things about ourselves through these moments. Even though I have a lot of training as a psychologist in so many of the areas my family struggled with, I needed to go through my own process of grief, questioning, and learning how to navigate different systems in both the parent and spouse role. In doing so, my compassion for and understanding of what my clients and parents experienced during the pandemic and beyond were deepened, and I hope that as a result, I have been able to bring more wisdom to the support I offer others.

My heart breaks when I see some of the scars left behind from the pandemic. I see kids worrying that something else could come out of the blue and completely change their lives without any warning or sense of control. We parents desperately want to keep our kids feeling emotionally safe and nurture their self-esteem. We recognize the constant tug-of-war with social media and our fight against diminished influence over our kids. I find that I often hold on too tight, trying to advocate for the girls and make sure they're cared for. I need to remember that when I let go of some of this, it helps build their sense of self-efficacy and resilience. I know that my parenting has evolved from having gone through the traumatic moments with my daughters, both difficult times resulting from the pandemic and difficult times that have had nothing to do with it. But still, letting go is so hard!

It is important to build in self-reflection and remind ourselves how far we have come. We need to make space for joy! This can be difficult to do but it is critical for our emotional well-being and resilience. Many parents feel guilty for having fun given what their child or teen is going through, but lightening up actually helps us and our children. We need to recharge with activities that nurture us to have the energy to keep going.

We also need to let go of what could have been. It is like assimilating a new part of ourselves, maybe even creating an updated vision of our families. We need to embrace our new reality and consciously choose how we want it to evolve by developing new outlets and ways to contribute and grow. As part of that process, we can create our own nurturing, supportive networks. Russell Moore stated, "Hope grows in community." It is important that we have friends and family who truly understand and can cry with us, build us up, support us, and pray with us. There is also room for friends who are removed from the situation as well and can help us feel a sense of identity outside of the trauma. Life will continue to present us with new challenges, and sometimes we will be truly blindsided. But, we can rest in the hope that we will not be forever knocked down. We can become stronger and more skillful as each wave hits (2024).

Going back to my daughter, Jules, I want to conclude with a message of hope. Jules has endured many challenges, hearing loss, multiple surgeries, celiac disease, injuries due to her celiac, and emotional difficulty and isolation during the pandemic. I interviewed my own daughter about her life trajectory for this section, and below I share what she experienced in her own words and what she has learned from these challenges.

Jules discussed that she does not have many memories about her hearing loss. She remembered picking out fancy sparkly hearing aids and she loved wearing them. On the negative side, she recalled getting "kicked out" of her preschool classroom for humming. She remembers that she would hum in order to feel "safe" and calm since there were so many amplified sounds in the classroom. She recalls her colorful ear plugs that she had to wear in her ears along with a swimming cap so that she did not get water in her ears, which could get to her open ear drums. She does not remember any of this slowing her down. Later on, Jules talked about feeling utter joy when she learned that her eardrums were healing and then, finally, when the second eardrum fully healed.

With regard to her celiac diagnosis, Jules remembers that it was confusing and scary. After the endoscopy, she recalls going to Whole Foods with Matt and me and we bought a lot of new gluten-free food. She asked for bagels, but we told her she couldn't eat regular bagels anymore. Of course, we learned a lot later about gluten-free foods and have found great gluten-free bagels! Jules described hating having celiac and being frustrated that she could not eat "all of the best things." She remembered feeling left out at birthday parties and classroom parties. Even though I would try to plan ahead of time to have the exact same flavor of gluten-free cupcake as the birthday cake at a party, or very similar gluten-free snacks during a classroom party, Jules remembers feeling different than everyone else.

Jules discussed her experience during the pandemic and described it as "awful." She missed her whole freshman year in high school. She commented that she still felt like a freshman in her sophomore year and likewise a year behind socially and emotionally during her junior year and senior year. She said that she wished she had been in elementary school during the pandemic since perhaps that would have been an easier time to go through it. Ultimately, Jules missed a quarter of her in-person high school experience and felt that was a loss of one of her "core years."

Jules has learned different things through all of these challenges. With celiac disease, she has grown to accept it and know she will have it forever. In terms of the pandemic, she realized how much of an extrovert she was and that she can't be away from people. She commented, "Everyone went crazy after the shutdown was over and we were with our friends so much. We were socially unaware of how to talk to people but had the desire to hang out with them anyway." Jules learned that she truly loves to be around people and how human interaction is an important part of the development of adolescents. She wondered if she would have been more mature if she had a normal freshman year of high school. But, she quickly noted that it doesn't feel good to feel sorry for yourself, and you need to stay productive and positive.

Now that Jules is in her sophomore year at a prestigious music conservatory for college in New York City, she described that it feels "amazing!" It is what she has wanted her whole life, and she has been constantly performing since kindergarten. If Jules had not had her eardrums heal, and instead had to have the risky surgery, she may never have been able to reach this goal. Since her eardrums healed, she has been blessed with perfect pitch, which is unbelievable for someone who had moderate to severe hearing loss!

When it comes to her drive and ambition, Jules described feeling scared that she was going to lose interest and not pursue singing and music. But, she quickly realized, "That's not me." She made a promise to herself that she would pursue this dream. Now she is going to a school that she wanted to go to since 8th grade. After a very arduous process of college applications, music applications, video pre-screen auditions and finally in-person auditions, she was accepted to a top music conservatory. It was confirmation for her that she was good enough to do this as a career. She finds it to be "so cool that I am pursuing this since it's what I wanted to do since I was a little girl!"

Ultimately, Jules has noticed that the best things happen to those who work the hardest and who are the most positive. She is a very positive person and stated that you need to pursue what you love and push until you get there. "When times get hard, people say that this is going to be too hard. But, I just say, ok, I am still going to do it." Jules stated that we all have those times where we don't see an end to it and everything seems to be going badly. "It may be hard to see the light, but it is always there. God gives you a plan that it's all going to work out but you have to trust the process. You have to keep pushing and don't let that hard time defeat you. If you really love what you're doing and love yourself, you won't be defeated."

References

Abeles, Vicki and Congdon, Jessica. (2010) The Race to Nowhere. Produced by Reel link Films: Lafayette, CA.

Anderson, Frank (2023) <u>Internal Family Systems Skills Training Manual: Trauma-Informed Treatment for Anxiety, Depression, PTSD & Substance Abuse</u>. Eau Claire, WI: PESI Publishing and Media.

Becker, Ernest (1975). <u>The Denial of Death</u>. p. 353. New York, NY: Free Press.

Boss, Pauline (2002). <u>Ambiguous Loss: Learning to Live With Unresolved Grief</u>. Boston, MA: Harvard University Press

Brazelton, T. Berry (1992). <u>Touchpoints: The Essential Reference</u>. Reading, MA: Addison-Wesley.

Brazelton, T. Berry & Sparrow, Joshua (2003). The Touchpoints Model of Development. Boston, MA: Brazelton Touchpoints Center.

Cleave, Chris (2010). <u>Little Bee</u>. pp. 8-9. New York, NY: Simon and Schuster.

Greenspan, Stanley and Wieder, Serena. (2009). <u>Engaging Autism: Using the Floortime Approach to Help Children, Relate, Communicate and Think</u>. Philadelphia, PA: Da Capo Lifelong Book.

Hendrix, Ryan, Palmer, Kari Zweber, Tarshis, Nancy, & Garcia, Michelle (2013). <u>We Thinkers Book Series</u>. Boston, MA:

Keller, Timothy. (2011) <u>The Meaning of Marriage: Facing the Complexities of Commitment with the Wisdom of God</u>. Grand Rapids, Michigan: Zondervan.

Kubler-Ross, Elizabeth (1969). <u>On Death and Dying</u>. New York: The Macmillan Company.

Kvist A.P., Nielsen H.S., Simonsen M. (2013). The importance of children's ADHD for parents' relationship stability and labor supply. *Social Science Medicine* 2013; 88:30–38.

Lamia, Mary C. (2011). The Power of Hope, and Recognizing When It's Hopeless. *Psychology Today.*

Levine, Madeline. (2008) <u>The Price of Privilege: How Parental Pressure and Material Advantage Are Creating a Generation of Disconnected and Unhappy Kids.</u> New York, NY: Harper.

Livneh, H., & Antonak, R. F. (1997). <u>Psychosocial adaptation to chronic illness and disability</u>. Boston, MA: Aspen Publishers.

Moore, Russell, David French & Curtis Chang. The After Party (2024). Produced by Redeeming Babel.

Murthy, Vivek (2024). Parents Under Pressure: The U.S. Surgeon General's Advisory on the Mental Health and Well-Being of Parents. *Office of the Surgeon General.* Washington, D.C.: US Department of Health and Human Services.

Resch, Aaron, Geraldo Mireles, Michael Benz, Cheryl Grenwelge, Rick Peterson and Dalun Zhang (2018). Giving Parents a Voice: A Qualitative Study of the Challenges Experienced by Parents of Children with Disabilities (p. 223-243). <u>The Psychological and Social Impact of Illness and Disability.</u> New York: Springer Publishing.

Schwartz, Richard (1997). <u>Internal Family Systems Therapy.</u> New York, NY: Guilford Press.

Schwartz, Richard. (2021). <u>No Bad Parts: Healing Trauma and Restoring Wholeness with the Internal Family Systems Model.</u> Boulder, CO: Sounds True.

Schwartz, Richard (2022). Internal Family Systems Therapy. Psychology Today.

Snyder, C. R., Harris, C., Anderson, J. R., and Holleran, S.A. (1991). Will and the Ways: Development and Validation of Individual-Differences Measure of Hope. *Journal of Personality and Social Psychology.* 60, pp. 570-585.

Tanna, Ravina J., Jerry W. Lin, and Orlando de Jesus. (2023). Sensorineural Hearing Loss. *National Institutes of Health.* Treasure Island, FL: StatsPearls Publishing.

Yoho, Sarah, Tyson Barrett, and Stephanie Borrie. (2023). The Influence of Sensorineural Hearing Loss on the Relationship Between the Perception of Speech in Noise and Dysarthric Speech. *Journal of Speech, Language and Hearing Research.* 66:10, pp. 4025-4036.

Parent Resource Websites

www.parentcenterhub.org/iep.
Center for Parent Information and Resources. This is the central hub of valuable information and products specifically designed for the network of Parent Centers serving families of children with disabilities. They provide parent information and resources as they go through the IEP process. Centers are located all over the United States.

www.autismspeaks.org/autism-support-family-help
Autism Speaks. National organization that provides tools, advocacy, research and support for family members of children, teens and adults with autism.

www.p2pusa.org.
Parent to Parent USA. A national support network to ensure access to quality emotional support for families of individuals with disabilities and/or special health care needs.

Acknowledgments

I am grateful to my family and friends who supported me throughout this process with their encouragement and faith in me. I am thankful to my husband, Matt, who believed in this book before I really knew how to write it. Your support, encouragement and suggestions have been incredibly important to me. Thank you to my beautiful daughters who were my inspiration for this book. This is my love letter to each of you. It has been the privilege of my life to be your mom. Thank you also to my parents, Dermot and Joy Rigg, for your encouragement and excitement about this book. Thank you to my in-laws, Rob and Barb Crossland, who always enjoyed discussing it.

Thank you to my friends who believed in this project. I appreciate all of the people I interviewed for this book and your input and contribution. Thank you to Dr. Kathryn Stewart for your contribution and interview. Thank you to my friend, Laura Shumaker, who spent time helping me imagine this book and to my colleague, Dr. Kent Grelling, who encouraged me to write it. Thank you to my writing coach, Cynthia Leslie-Bole, who helped me in this journey and always inspired me to keep going and tell my story. Finally thank you to my publisher, Karen Mireau Rimmer, for taking a chance on this special book.

I also want to thank all of the professionals, doctors, therapists and teachers who have helped and advocated for our daughters over the years. Thank you to Carol Goodman, Janet Gordon, Lorraine Palizza, Ann Grundstein, Karen Acrish, Izabela Swiecka, Sandra Delgado, Dr. Robert Wesman, Dr. Anna Messner, Dr. Nisha Khavari, Lesa Swiatlowicz, Kathy Miller, Olivia Vann, Deborah Hungerford, Jennifer Girard, Krystal Alderete, Jeff Hutson, Judy Bensinger-Haynes, Dr. Adrienne Candell, and Dr. Elizabeth Burns Kramer. Finally, thank you to my dear friend, Jen Bielawski, who helped me discover and understand celiac disease for Jules. You have all played important roles in my daughters' lives and have touched their lives forever.

—Jennifer Crossland
November, 2025

About the Author

Jennifer Crossland has always been fascinated by human behavior and drawn to helping others. She received her Bachelor of Arts in psychology from Baylor University. Then she earned a Master of Science in rehabilitation counseling psychology and a Ph.D in clinical psychology from the University of Texas Southwestern Medical Center at Dallas.

Jennifer then studied and trained in a post-doctoral fellowship at Boston Children's Hospital. During this fellowship, she specialized in evaluation and treatment of children with developmental disabilities and mental health concerns. Subsequently, she worked in a therapeutic preschool program for children on the autism spectrum at Texas Children's Hospital in Houston.

Jennifer started her private practice in Westchester County, New York, where she was also on faculty at New York Medical College conducting seminars on autism for residents and fellows. Her practice consisted of providing psychological evaluations, supportive play and behavior therapy for young children, and cognitive behavioral therapy for grade-school age children and adolescents.

In 2010, Jennifer and her family relocated to Lafayette, California, in the San Francisco Bay Area where she continued to work in private practice, counseling and advocating for children, teens and young adults.

Jennifer loves to spend time with family and friends, cooking, writing, hiking, going on walks with her dog, and traveling with her husband, Matt, and her three beautiful daughters.

To Contact the Author:
Instagram@jennifercrossland.books
drcrossland@comcast.net
www.drcrossland.com

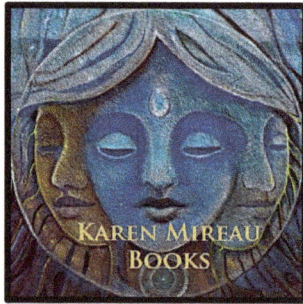

To Contact the Publisher
KarenMireauBooks@gmail.com
www.KarenMireauBooks.com

For Direct Book Orders:
Lulu.com/shop